ADORNO:
AN INTRODUCTION

Other Works in
The Pennbridge Introductory Series

Foucault   by Hinrich Fink-Eitel
Habermas   by Detlef Horster

ADORNO:
AN INTRODUCTION

Willem van Reijen
with contributions by
Peter Schiefelbein and
Hans-Martin Lohmann

Translated from the German
by Dieter Engelbrecht

Pennbridge Books
Philadelphia

Pennbridge Books, March 1992
Translation copyright ©1992 by Pennbridge Communications Inc.

All rights reserved under International and Pan-American Copyright
Conventions. Published in the U.S. by Pennbridge Communications Inc.
Originally published in Germany as Adorno zur Einführung by Junius Verlag
GmbH (Hamburg).
Copyright 1990

Library of Congress Catalog Card Number
92-60243

Design and Typesetting: Falco & Falco Incorporated
Printing: Versapress

Manufactured in the United States
ISBN 1-880055-00-7

CONTENTS

Editor's Note: When a work has been translated into English the English title is used. Otherwise the title will appear in German, French etc.

The Publisher would like to thank Jean Stearns, Rod Coghlan and Gordon Yee for their assistance in the preparation of this volume.

PREFACE TO THE AMERICAN EDITION

The only philosophy which can be responsibly practiced in [the] face of despair is the attempt to contemplate all things as they would present themselves from the standpoint of redemption. . . . Perspectives must be fashioned that displace and estrange the world, reveal it to be, with its rifts and crevices, as it will appear one day in the messianic light. To gain such perspectives without velleity or violence, entirely from felt contact with its objects — this alone is the task of thought. (from T. Adorno *Minima Moralia*, trans. by E.F.N. Jephcott)

Perhaps the greatest lesson we can learn from Adorno is that what we know as "culture" is neither something to take for granted nor something which we can or should consume passively. Whether we are talking about history, science, language or art the challenge is to literally take these things apart, to view the inner dynamics and mechanics of these phenomena and to locate them in their specific socio-historical contexts.

Like all perspicacious modernists Adorno was aware of how the "commodification" of culture has become an increasingly unpleasant side-effect of public life in the 20th century. For this reason Adorno chose a style of philosophizing that he himself likened to "a stick in the eye." While this style may have prevented Adorno's thoughts from being "passively consumed," it has also made it difficult for Adorno's works to receive the size of audience he might otherwise have garnered had he made some deference to straight-forwardness (or even basic clarity). It also has not helped that Adorno has not always been adequately served by the translators of his major works, thus compounding an already difficult problem.

As the inaugural work in the new Pennbridge Introductory Series, this study by Willem van Reijen should add to our understanding of Adorno, particularly as it illuminates the difficult discussion on the relationships between philosophy and history as well as philosophy and science. Two other contributors, Peter Schiefelbein and Hans-Martin Lohmann, respectively add their thoughts on two of Adorno's major works, *Negative Dialectics* and *Aesthetic Theory*. Together, these three scholars give us a unique European perspective on Adorno's major ideas and hopefully will help to make the profound insights of this gifted, troubled man more widely understood by a no less troubled *fin de siécle* audience.

—The Editors

CHAPTER

1

THE PHILOSOPHICAL PROGRAM IN ADORNO'S EARLY ESSAYS

Adorno's first philosophical works, the dissertation *Die Transzendenz des Dinglichen und Noëmatischen in Husserls Phänomenologie* from 1924 and his work *Der Begriff des Unbewußten in der transzendentalen Seelenlehre* from the year 1927 are still very much influenced by Husserl's phenomenology as it was represented to Adorno by his mentor Cornelius. However, Adorno's commencement speech from the year 1931 *Die Aktualität der Philosophie* and *Die Idee der Naturgeschichte*, which was written a year later, show a much different Adorno.

From 1927 Adorno's thinking was more recognizably influenced by Walter Benjamin (they had met for the first time around 1922)[1]. Adorno had read Benjamin's works about Goethe's *Wahlverwandschaften* and about the *Ursprung des deutschen Trauerspiels* and he was especially impressed by Benjamin's thoughts on the importance of "pictures."

Benjamin understood reality as a universe of elements which, in our perception of them, compose "pictures." For Benjamin, our perception of reality is always an interpretation, an order constituting activity—performed by the subject—in which disparate elements compose one meaningful total picture. Benjamin's considerations, however, attempted to show that reality in-itself is not an orderly entirety. He takes into account that our perception is, in fact, socio-historically overdetermined and that common notions about perception are erroneous. Through the routine and unquestioning perception of reality we forget that perception is an active, subjective and orderly effort that attributes meaning. We also forget that we tend to remain at one level of routine perceptions which no longer agree with experiences at other levels or which are basically "wrong."

Adorno was fascinated by Benjamin's theory that only our mental processing, our perception of reality, can grant order to this reality and thus provide its meaning. He believed that philosophy's main responsibility is to attribute a new order to the pictures that have been formed throughout our cultural development. According to Adorno, a new order is necessary because our culture displays symptoms of decay which, in his view, continue to increase in dramatic fashion.

In reviewing Adorno's works from his commencement speech to the *Negative Dialectics* we see a steady development and variation of this initial concept in his philosophy. This does not imply, however, that Adorno's later works are only repeated versions of earlier theories. Adorno's philosophy is, like almost no other contemporary philosophy, rich with the most diverse and exciting perspectives; but clearly his *leitmotif* is the new order of our perceptions and experiences.

Furthermore, Adorno's work—in this regard probably only comparable to the other philosophers of the Frankfurt School—shows a remarkable continuity in perspective and subject when compared to his contemporaries. This is not to say that continuity alone is a measure for judging philosophical quality, but still, the continuity of a social philosophy is meaningful when it claims to contribute its share to the understanding of its time, and where it recognizes that social science cannot be separated from its social function, in other words, that the separation of scientific and philosophical approaches on the one hand, and of the subject to be defined on the other, is fiction. The more history claims autonomy and secludes itself from changes, and the more people are unwilling to form their own history in a conscious and self-determined way, the more it is that philosophy must face this problem and determine its consequences.

What can be changed is the constituted order of our pictures of the world which must be renewed repeatedly. Constantly renewing the order of pictures may loosen indifferent patterns of perception and experience and thus make clear that history is paralyzed and has withdrawn itself from methodological and rational influences by man. It may also make clear that our very "knowledge" has turned to stone.

Adorno views his philosophy as a denial of this torpidity, as an evolving negative criticism which suggests that the current state of reality is "wrong" and should be changed.

I will explain Adorno's intention and his philosophical approaches in the following paragraphs referring to his commencement speech and to the above mentioned lecture *Die Idee der Naturgeschichte*.

THE ACTUALITY OF PHILOSOPHY

Philosophy can no longer assume that it will encompass reality in its entirety. This assumption became an illusion after the catastrophe of the First World War which shocked many scientists and philosophers and shook their faith in the world-improving function of science. Adorno came to a radical conclusion and stated that practically every attempt to be rational is doomed to fail. The totally desolate situation of society and our culture denies philosophy even the possibility for rational criticism. Philosophy, in a traditional sense, turns necessarily into a justification of the existing situation. This objectivizing function of philosophy has become increasingly clear in society, yet many philosophers still remain blind towards barbarity and injustice. Aiming at Heidegger, who had published *Being and Time* in 1927 and gained great influence as a result, Adorno remarked that it had obviously become possible now to introduce absolutely radical, but, (despite their apparent radicalism,) also unfounded questions such the question about "Being". Philosophy helps in this way to disguise the real misery and simultaneously deceives everybody about its actual questions.

To specify this questioning one must "brush history the wrong way," as Benjamin says. The development of society is headed for a total integration of any criticism. Anything that does not maintain, expand and increase the existing order is threatened by downfall and philosophy must also bend to the demands of this development. The main reason, according to Adorno, is that logic, mathematics and the natural sciences have became dominant and their exemplary model and dominance of the material sphere has succeeded as a model for scientism in general. The "reality" of the positive sciences does not represent a coherent entirety. Individual sciences always provide only segmental pictures, single facts and laws of limited validity; yet they understand this limited perspective and everything seen under this perspective as the entirety. This isolates not only moments of reality, which truly form an entirety, but simultaneously it isolates their own movement away from reality.

The intention of a critical philosophy is to retrieve "the abundance of material and specific problems" from the individual sciences and it must oppose their prerogative to define what can be called "reality." Unlike science, critical philosophy does not intend to inflate the capacity of its categories to a higher level, as many claim it does. Adorno writes:

> There is a clear difference: an individual science accepts its findings, especially its most profound and latest findings, as unresolvable and imperturbable, while philosophy understands the originally encountered finding as a sign that must be deciphered. In simple words: the idea of science is research, the idea of philosophy is interpretation.[2]

Philosophy has no predetermined approach for interpretation; the subject to be interpreted—namely all human activities—also includes philosophical consideration. Likewise one can say that every philosophical understanding offers a different view of the entire picture. In other words: we must also determine the means of determination. Philosophy must define itself. To define "interpretation" is also a question of interpretation. This doesn't necessarily lead us into a dreaded logical circle (and thus to a great philosophical effort) because logic in itself also works only in segments. Furthermore, to address the limited range of logic does not naturally imply that it is wide open to contradictions, as we like to assume. First we have to question whether logic can establish science as a theory of the entirety. This question must be denied: logic proceeds from assumptions that it cannot determine logically in itself. Therefore, logic requires a philosophical justification of its doings.

Adorno tries to bring all disparate moments of the existing culture into a new order. He wants to bestow true meaning and function to particular moments of our social reality regarding art, economics and science. This may be deceiving at first glance as these activities exist only by themselves and seemingly follow different laws, while in reality, they are connected to one another. Adorno defines this interconnection in a formula that, today, reminds us of structuralism: he calls it a puzzle or text that has to be deciphered. "Interpreting philosophy must construe keys that open reality."[3] Also part of this complex reality is the history of philosophy. If philosophy writes its own history then we again encounter the problem of proof: philosophy ought to be text and decoding of text in one.

Although Adorno uses the term "text" we should remember Benjamin's influence and therefore rather think of "pictures." A "picture" comprises more possible human experiences and ways of experiencing than the term "text" can suggest and, in fact, Adorno thinks of picturing as the most complete activity possible to reorganize our experience of the empirical world. He outlines a task sharing between the special branches of science and philosophy, yet, one without a strictly predetermined structure. The function of philosophy is always to interrelate results and views of the special sciences; the picture of the entirety will change constantly—so will the moments that form the entirety—always taking on new forms.

It is important to realize that Adorno intends to criticize existing circumstances without comparing them to the idea of a better world. This would be useless to the existing world. Adorno specifically draws the line at questions related to the meaning of human existence (such as found in Heidegger's "existentialism") or regarding a "world behind the world" (Husserl). It is not a function of philosophy to interpret reality as "meaningful" or to ascribe to it hidden intentions,

> but to interpret reality without intentions . . . interpretation of the unintended through the collection of analytically isolated elements and the exposure of reality due to such interpretation: this is the program of every real materialistic perception.[4]

It is Adorno's intention to call his approach "materialistic" since it proceeds from the existing situation and not from an a priori understanding of the "essential." The configuring moments of this situation confront one another in different ways so that they must disclose themselves as what they truly are. This is not a singular event: the new order must not be paralyzed, it must be constantly rewritten and carried forward. Reality as "unintended" implies that the meaning of moments which form reality is neither decided in the past nor will it be disclosed in the future. It only exists with single moments relating to each other in the here and now, thus forming the entire social reality. The fact that Adorno places the meaning of moments of the social reality in the "here and now" does not imply that he has lost perspective for the past and future. Yet, the question as to the origin of any meaning is different from the question as to the actual functions of defined social phenomena.

Adorno will pursue the question of origins in his later work; but even then the present remains his predominant viewpoint. He looks back to the past and investigates those moments that today display symptoms of decay in the context of our social order and cultural development. Adorno proves that these moments have an early origin; this becomes especially clear in his *Dialectic of Enlightenment* which he wrote together with Horkheimer. Adorno justifies the priority of the "present" and the way we experience it; while choosing a perspective on the past or the future could lead to selective perceptions. Thus we can easily select a way of life that we perceive subjectively as "good" and one which we believe had been real in the past (such as Hegel found the perception of the Greek *polis* to be enticing); or we might even imagine other forms of society which we might contrast to the present situation. This leads to a subjectively prejudiced view of the present situation which does not agree with philosophical analysis.

Adorno's philosophy can intentionally be called materialistic and also historical because it accounts for both perspectives. In so far as it follows, not only these but other intentions will be discussed later. However, I would like to point out that the approach to the historical in Adorno's philosophy (and also its dialectics, as we will show) comes to a "standstill." When we concentrate on the present situation and take the categories of interpretation exclusively from the present time, we run the risk that certain elements of the past will fall through the screen of this perception. When we take moments that don't become historically effective until a later time, and when we concentrate only on the present time, then we might lose the view of developing dynamics. In the case where Adorno's philosophy results in a standstill of dialectics one must ask whether this is the result of his concept of "unintended reality."

Yet Adorno's attacks on traditional philosophy aim especially at its teleological concept. He then combines these assaults against teleological philosophy with one against relativizing philosophy as a "system." The complete world-picture (*Weltbild*), that goes hand in hand with the attempted designing of a definite order of all phenomena, suggests to Adorno that philosophy has untied itself from a reality that constantly changes and that it has taken refuge in abstractions. Adorno tries to explain that philosophy must constantly form new relations among the elements of an existing order. Accordingly, philosophy should not view reality in an abstract way, nor should it add anything.

Adorno suggests that the construction of reality from disparate elements requires that philosophy

> . . . abandons the grand problems whose scope has endeavored to guarantee totality, while nowadays "interpretation" slips through the wide meshes of the net. If interpretation is truly a collection of the smallest elements then it no longer participates in grand problems in a traditional sense but only in a way that denies the total question in specific areas that were once apparently represented symbolically.[5]

If philosophy wants to understand the existing reality as is, it must first do an inventory and "untie itself from the world as it appears," as Adorno once remarked in respect to a similar demand by Freud for psychoanalysis. In such a situation the "tendency of progressive social philosophy towards economics"[6] is not only a result of the overpowering economic sector in society but also a result of the immanently necessary analysis of facts that must form the basis of any philosophy.

Analysis of consumption shows us that an interpretation of society must be performed in terms of conflicting interests. Conflicting interests indicate that the whole in which they originate and develop is not a true whole. As long as this is true everything must be understood in terms of conflict, which means in regard to an opponent. Nothing can be understood by and of "itself." This concludes that philosophy neither understands reality in its intention nor even enough of itself. In a disparate reality philosophy also remains a conglomerate of disparate moments.

Being aware of that gives reason enough to suspect that reality could be different. Adorno sees herein the chance to understand philosophy as a proven possibility to "be different." The "different" order of social elements does not stop at the imagination but constitutes—as philosophy—part of reality. At this turning point philosophy can free itself from its involvement with the existing reality and can prove that there is no true separation of social elements (i.e. economics and philosophy). Furthermore, the so-called "ivory tower" (*Weltfremdheit*) of philosophy becomes a measure of its "truth": the torn curtain of reality has given the appearance of an entirety, but now even single moments may show their true reality. With this the beginning of changes have penetrated reality.

Only when we eliminate the distance between philosophy and reality can philosophy find itself. When the entirety of reality and philosophy are truly themselves then it is possible that philosophy will tell the truth about reality. Agreeing with Marx, Adorno believes that suspending "bad reality" will also suspend "bad philosophy." He gives neither one of them priority; their configuration includes the alteration of one moment causing a change in the other. Adorno describes his thoughts in detail in *Die Idee der Naturgeschichte*.

THE IDEA OF NATURAL HISTORY

In his lecture *Die Idee der Naturgeschichte* Adorno explains the difference between traditional philosophy and his own approach. As I have mentioned before Adorno believes that traditional philosophy, no less than the individual sciences, has lost view of the grand picture of social developments and relations. Without overlapping analysis only segmented aspects are examined. But even these cannot be adequately understood any longer since the relations between the partial aspects and the whole are seen in an abstract way. Yet, it is especially these relations that develop each segment of the whole. In science the segments are isolated and this has a direct effect on what we believe we know about these partial aspects and even on our understanding of knowledge in general. Detailed knowledge appears as scientific, yet each view of the grand picture is suspected of being ideology or speculation. In his lecture, that we'll examine now more closely, Adorno will argue exactly that this seemingly scientific knowledge of details is empty speculation and fulfills an ideological function regarding its specific contents and also regarding the understanding of science that is derived from it. Adorno levels his charges against traditional philosophy in his dispute with the young Scheler and also the phenomenologists Husserl and Heidegger, whom he considers typical representatives of philosophical history. Adorno believes that they carry developments in the tradition to extremes. In his view this is also proof for the untenability of their assumptions.

These unproven claims are exactly reflected in our understanding of history, according to Adorno. Traditionally, we see history as something concluded and unchangeable, as a "fact." Our knowledge of historical facts is also unchangeable (at least when we know all the factors). Known facts and knowledge account evenly as predetermined dimensions. Adorno calls it the ontologizing of history and its knowledge. The criterion of unchangeability becomes, consciously or subconsciously, a criterion for the reliability of our specific knowledge and with that a criterion for our knowledge per se. With that the unchangeable is synonymous with the essential and the changeable is synonymous with the accidental. Traditional philosophy specifies its understanding of knowledge and philosophy: it accepts only the knowledge of the unchangeable as true knowledge.

Our understanding of history has also fallen victim—according to Adorno—to the tendency to match the recognizable with the unchangeable. Adorno does not believe, of course, that one could subsequently change historical facts. He wants to state that historical facts are especially and always subject to interpretation.

Whether we call an armed dispute a battle or not, depends, of course, on whether we view or don't view certain sequences as historically important; whether we attribute a certain continuity to history and whether we therefore accept an understanding of historical continuity at all. Adorno believes that we do it in respect to every single event in history and that we can't do anything else but to constantly interject this continuity into history. That again implies that we've always proceeded from our actual experience, namely from the meaning we attribute to specific moments. Adorno concludes from it that history is and must be subject to constant interpretation or otherwise the connection between our actual situation and our history would be lost. He charges individual sciences (not only history but also natural sciences and, beyond that, philosophy) with becoming slaves to an understanding of history that presents history as mere accumulation of facts. With that history becomes paralyzed as something unchangeable which is then suspended from interpretation because of actual [historical] experience.

The primacy of the unchangeable is also analogically important for its perception. To recognize the unchangeable is considered the highest form of human perception. This knowledge will remain the same and finally even decide the meaning of "knowledge" itself. In this way, says Adorno, history and knowledge will be absolutely separated from one another. Each moment forms a reality for itself; each one of them is unchangeable, based in itself, and cannot be reached by another moment. Adorno aims his criticism exactly against this paralysis of history and perception in singling them out and comparing them to one another. In a later quote he remarks: "The truth does not lie in history, as relativism demands, but history lies in the truth." Transferring the focal point in this thesis should not mislead us to believe that Adorno considers history and its interpretation equal, which we will explain in detail later. Yet criticism of tradition forces us to go to extremes because tradition itself takes everything to an extreme.

Adorno wants to show that history and perception cannot be viewed separately from one another. Our knowledge is historical, our history is only what we recognize as such. Views of history and perception simply depend on one another. In losing sight of it we also lose the understanding that everything we call "history" also determines essentially our view of true history (specific important events, continuity, etc.) The relation between history and knowledge must therefore be viewed as a relation of reciprocal constitution. It is important then that we don't isolate this reciprocity again and thus introduce a new ontology.

In questioning the relation of nature and history Adorno intends

> to annul the common antithesis of nature and history . . . to drive these two terms to a point where they annul themselves into actually falling apart.[8]

Thus he eliminates the possibility that the idea of natural history could be anticipated as a unity. For the time being both terms should rather be handled as a problem posed by idealistic philosophy to separate the natural (in a "differential procedure") from the illusion of a non-authentic history and to reconstruct real history as a way of being and as a "motion of nature."[9] Dialectical views should lead to a certain terminology which approximates facticity; where one can recognize the inversion of reality for which ontological theories offer only philosophical formulas and exaggerations, but not at all real insight.

Adorno's understanding of "nature" disagrees with the understanding of nature generated by the natural sciences. When Adorno distances himself per definition from the natural view of the natural sciences it is not from a condescending attitude. Adorno takes the definitions of the special sciences into account but he argues that they fall short.

Adorno views nature not only as "matter" with all its identified laws but also as an expression, particularly, of the "singularity" of everything that exists. Therefore Adorno emphasizes the incomparable individuality of every existing being. He criticizes the indifferent view that is handed down to us from the views of natural science. In experiments, for example, natural science doesn't care very much about a specific rabbit or atom. Each one of them is as good or bad as the other. Individual matter and individuality cannot emerge at all—science is only interested in the characteristics of the species. This indifference is also reflected on the part of the observing and researching subject. It absolutely doesn't matter who performs the experiment and its calculation. This mutual indifference expresses itself in the views of science and in the curious perception of its social neutrality or objectivity. Individual and group interests don't appear at all; if they nevertheless do so, then they are on forbidden grounds.

In his view of nature, Adorno very much emphasizes the perspective of individuality and also the singularity of all living things. He also targets the neglected historical dimension of natural existence and especially of individual beings. Individual "matter" can only be understood if it has a history, and thus it must also exist as historical matter. On the other hand, historic dimensions can only be truly experienced by individual things. This is analogically valid for nature and history. He concludes that the moments called nature and history do not merge but simultaneously fall apart and cross each other in a way

> that the natural appears as a sign for history and history as sign for nature.[10]

The reciprocity of nature and history is, according to Adorno, expressed in "interpretation." Interpretation emphasizes things in nature that have gone out of sight from natural science; the historical aspect of the natural and, regarding history, things that had been forgotten in the studies of history, namely that history becomes reality in a natural environment. Both moments undergo a metamorphosis when interpreted, and everything changes, including our perception of the moments and the entirety of which it is a part. "Nature *itself* presents itself as transient nature, as

history"[11] and "historical existence is, in its most extreme, historical definition where it is closest to understanding itself as natural existence."[12]

Adorno wants to revive the concepts that have practically
become indifferent in the sciences so he can also change reality
that has been practically predetermined through these indifferent concepts. The indifference of concepts becomes apparent in
the definitional separation of things which *au fond* form a unity.
It also indicates that we truly don't use our thinking any longer
and therefore don't take the reciprocal changes of moments into
account. In addition, we have lost insight and understanding of
reality and thought that stipulate and change each other. There
is no Archimede's Law in which reality can stipulate thought, or
vice versa, or in which either one could be understood. Our understanding is, therefore, not a constant factor, not a *fundamentum inconcussum* of eternally valid logical operations to which
we could submit reality.

This reciprocal stipulation of nature and history, of understanding and reality, again, must not be seen as a firm and therefore abstract relation. It is subject to a historic development which
we ourselves also experience and which will manifest itself only
objectively. This exchange of information itself is seen historically.

> Every separation of natural statics from historical dynamics leads
> to absolutely wrong terms; each separation of historical dynam-
> ics from the natural, irreversibly defined in it, leads to bad spiritu-
> alism.[13]

Nature, history and thought form one unity that also appears
in every single moment. Nature is no less history than history
is nature—both are inherent to the process of thought. The process
of thought, however, should not evaluate the contents of truth
derived from the definitions of "true" and "false" that are offered
by traditional philosophy. Thought is truthful when the history
of our analyses and our perspective of nature are taken into account, and when neither of these perspectives demand priority

over the other. It is exactly this, in Adorno's view, that holds history together in its innermost core. Philosophy, in its self-definition, has always claimed to define itself autonomously; it then also defined, from within itself, everything else. Yet, though Adorno denies philosophy the right (and the ability) to define nature and history, it is still valid to say that nature and history cannot exist as they are if there is no true philosophy. If philosophy doesn't truly understand nature and history in their original unity they can't exist—if they form a unity with the process of thought at all—in this original unity.

This consideration leads time and again to misunderstandings when people read Adorno's works for the first time because it seemingly leads to contradictions. On the one hand, Adorno claims that traditional philosophy is untrue because it presents things in a wrong way, on the other hand he claims that it is true because it reflects actual events in a correct way. The paradox is solved if we don't define the terms "true" and "untrue" as strictly logical contradictions. Adorno can call traditional philosophy "true" in a sense that this stipulation is used by philosophy itself: as correct interpretation of the existing—*adaequatio*. It interprets exactly the definitional separation of nature and history and the factual results of the special sciences and their functions, each for itself and in society. But this is precisely Adorno's criticism and what he can call "untrue" or "true."

Adorno, therefore, doesn't use these terms within the framework of a truth theory to qualify judgments or "sentences" but uses them rather as terms indicating a "twisted" reality. The correct interpretation of a twisted reality can then simultaneously be called "true" and "untrue."

The untrue character of interpretation and subsequently the fact that reality is twisted are, according to Adorno, shaded by traditional philosophy in its aim toward existing being. Yet the term "being" is so vague that it comprises indiscriminately everything historical and also everything real. Therefore, philosophy loses understanding and meaning of the historically different and the actually existing separations (as between nature and history). It also lacks the understanding that not everything existing exists as it determines itself—including philosophy; therefore, nothing is defined through its own existence; nothing is identical with itself.

Adorno does not take the perception "how things should be in their own existence" from "the outside." For history he develops the picture of history from itself: his definition of history includes nature and the processes of thought. Thus Adorno widens the common use of the term "history" which is, in respect to the individual sciences, too limited in its definition. Decisions about this definition are, of course, not only a question of definition. The question is how we perceive the relation between theory and practice and which theoretical and practical consequences we draw from our perception of history. For Adorno, this implies criticism of traditional philosophy because when we discuss the meaning of concepts in relation to the problem of history, we cannot rightfully assume that science is superior to philosophy, or vice versa. This also implies that philosophy cannot limit itself to problems of definition and methodology but that it must also point to practical aspects.

Although practice cannot be judged without theoretical perceptions, Adorno chose, for the time being, to leave his own perceptions out of the discussion. He examines the ways of true actions with principles stemming from science and philosophy. He finds that there is seldom agreement regarding reality or between reality and scientific and philosophical statements. This non-identity reveals itself, except in errors, specifically in the difference between alleged intentions of social conduct and reality. It is impossible to form a social reality so that it agrees with the ideas of science and philosophy. It is further impossible to guide reality with the tools of science and philosophy in respect to human goals; nor is it possible to describe reality in logical truth.

For the present, this statement is a *negativum*. Adorno develops his criticism from here; in doing so he avoids crossing the limits of experience. He states that reality is different from how we imagine it and he tries to grasp this difference as part of the situation and in commonly understood terms. The negative must be experienced and understood as part of the real situation. It is of the greatest importance for us to understand that Adorno does not at all consider the possibility that he could reach a total agreement (identity). He distances himself explicitly from contemporary ontology.

> The ontological claim to stand beyond the divergence of nature and history is derived surreptitiously . . . but ontology is bound to the ideological procedure, the reconciliation of the mind, because the real procedure failed.[14]

Yet, the concept of suspending the negative expresses itself in the perception that negativity is "bad reality." This determination of reality is, of course, not a moral condemnation but a qualification which should show that reality and our thoughts about reality do not agree; it should also show that we deceive ourselves constantly when we believe that we talk "about" reality.

This self-deception is developed in the fact that we still describe and explain reality as a picture of consistency and consequence to which we then add the claim of rationality, and therefore, the self-determination of any thought process. The process of thought, however, has no priority over reality in a sense that one could measure reality with the pretensions of logic. Because reality reveals itself as not "logical" and that things in themselves are not identical, it indicates that logic falls short. Reality itself makes us understand that its appearances do not agree with meanings and functions. That had been concluded by Adorno in his thoughts about nature and history.

These considerations are also the basis for the term "totality" which is often misunderstood by Adorno's critics. Adorno doesn't mystify the whole in a sense that it could be "more" than the sum of all segments. He refers to the "collapse of the last philosophical claims for totality" and "eliminating any concept of a self-sufficient totality of the mind,"[15] because these concepts are exactly those that fail before the non-identity of reality, i.e. philosophy and science—each for itself and in relation to each other. The moment of non-identity is part of everything existing and also part of all existence and our understanding of it.

Adorno, therefore, understands the term "totality" differently from traditional philosophy: it is the abundance of the existing and also the moment of non-being, or to be more precise—and to avoid any wrong associations with Heidegger—of the non-identical-being. Adorno, in contrast to Heidegger, doesn't ontologize this definition. The non-identical-being is not a definition that is indifferently valid for all phases of historic developments and everything else. It must be concretized in interlacing representation and criticism of the *existing with one another* because representation itself always introduces only the part of the entirety which can be expressed in rational terms. That this part is, however, not the entirety must be said in terms of this limited language. That leads seemingly to a contradiction. One makes a statement about reality and admits simultaneously that reality doesn't include everything that is stated.

This abstract presentation indicates that everything seems a mere philosophical problem. Yet, if we look at it more closely, we experience the familiar phenomenon that something that is forced into existence cannot be itself. The strictly logical separation of "yes" and "no" is not enough to account for this truth. Apparent logical contradictions express a deficit of reality itself. Philosophical criticism doesn't fall out of the skies and neither is it the sad business of certain hypochondriacs; it is rather the crying voice of a silent reality that is a permanent part of reality itself. If that part is missing, reality remains to achieve negativity. Wholeness and totality consist therefore of both components: of the existing in so far it realizes or can realize its potential; and of the potential that is not and cannot become reality and which would help the existing to find its true existence. These facts must be expressed in "criticism."

In his later work *Negative Dialectics*, we will see how Adorno tries to prove that "finding yourself" may be impossible under present conditions. Totality now and in the future will be dominated by the negative and philosophy can therefore only work as criticism. The deep discrepancy between philosophy as theory and practice becomes apparent. Philosophy cannot improve the situation under present circumstances. All it can do is reveal the inadequacies of our social order and express itself as criticism.

The term totality also implies resignation. Entirety, as it is, prevents self-realization: the appearance of nature does not at all reveal its own true existence. The traditional difference between essence and appearance has thus lost all its meaning. This doesn't [necessarily] force Adorno into agnosticism because he clings to the experience of objective situations. What remains to be proven is that history and nature lead to very contradictory concepts under the present conditions. The perception of these concepts reveals their dominant rationality which, on the other hand, questions again this dominance. The total separation of "true" and "false" will fail because of its prerequisite assumptions.

Adorno sees the origin of this development in the beginnings of our cultural heritage. His historical perspective finds the causes of today's negative experiences in the past. Adorno believes that the tendency that nothing existing can maintain its original "first" nature has already manifested itself in our earliest history.

Man creates myth to overcome his *angst* in the face of the uncertainties of natural influences. To dominate fear prevents fear from being what it truly is. Yet that puts control (*Herrschaft*) as the dominant behavior into reality. It (*Herrschaft*) adopts the form of (rational) explanation. The cultural institutionalizing of this second nature overwhelms all experience so that the understanding of the historic coherence will be lost in first "and" second nature. A certain "ordering" of our experience has the effect that reality can no longer appear outside this order. What we experience is defined by the order of experience. It is the task of naturo-historic thinking to break open this order of experience, permit a view of the destruction of first nature and to lead second nature back to its origin across the ruins of history. This philosophical effort is, according to Adorno, "immanent interpretation . . . of specific basic elements of the historical dialectic."[16]

Adorno and other members of the Institute for Social Research have often been criticized for having laid claim to the term "historical-materialism." Adorno believes without a doubt that his (negative) dialectics are a historical-materialistic theory. He believes it because his writings include history as well as its social circumstances and because he sees the development of his theory connected with cultural and political-economic developments. If we don't view dialectics as simply a method among other methods but understand that reality does not exist independently outside our perception of reality, then we can conclude that Adorno's philosophy is dialectic and thus historical-materialistic. However, one could prove that Adorno does not speak about the true social circumstances but only about his perception of these circumstances. (I'll come back to this thought later on).

What is the claim of the definition "historical-materialism?" Is it in accordance with Marx? The opinions about Marx's theory also differ wildly. That is not to say that Marx's theory had remained so imprecise that he could be interpreted in any given way; it is more that political interest and motive have let us choose this theory.

I therefore suggest to first define the term "dialectics." They are every theory with the premise that historical (cultural, social and political) development is the expression and consequence of a dispute between contradictory interests and the opinions linked to them.

Without doubt, we can call Adorno's philosophy dialectic in this regard. What has been created and developed by our culture is the discrepancy between our understanding of "nature" and "history," between reality and the thought which claims to rule reality. This discrepancy is a central theme of Adorno's philosophy and thus justifies the above conclusion. Because dialectics work in historical dimensions, one cannot deny Adorno's historical thinking. He reconstructs today's predominant "false appearance(s)" from "prehistoric" developments. In *Dialectic of Enlightenment* he and Horkheimer define Ulysses' cunning against the overpowering mystical figures as the foundation of modern individual self-consciousness.

Adorno's self-understanding as a materialistic philosopher is probably the hardest to defend here, if we intend to use the term "materialistic" only for those theories that define history as the history of class war (at least in the bourgeois period). However, Adorno views history as the history of the rational ruling over everything that it has defined itself; ruling over that which is different from itself (nature, feelings), over the human being as "natural being" (in regard to only himself), and over all other human beings in so far as they don't share my "rationale." Class war is a phenomenon for Adorno that is only one symptom among others of this ruling by rationale.[17]

CHAPTER

2

ADORNO'S CRITICISM OF TRADITIONAL PHILOSOPHY AS A THEORY OF COGNITION

According to Adorno, the preface to the paper *Against Episte-mology: A Metacritique* (1955/56), (subtitled "Studies in Husserl and the Phenomenological Antimonies") which, to a great extent, originated from his time in Oxford, forms, to some degree, along with *Der Essay als Form*,[18] the program of his philosophy.[19] Of similar rank is only the *Negative Dialectics*.

During his stay in Oxford Adorno decided to finally settle accounts with the "traditional philosophy" that he believed had deteriorated to a mere theory of cognition—as Husserl and Heidegger's phenomenology clearly demonstrate. This overdeveloped theory of cognition makes it possible to reveal this type of philosophy as a misdevelopment striving towards completion. Completion, in the dialectical sense, is also a suspension in a sense: to disappear at the zenith. Carried to extremes, philosophy suspends itself from its own trends. Yet, when a philosophy eliminates itself then its claim to truth the justification of philosophy—is deceptive. That is even more revealing since this traditional philosophy has founded its claim to truth on its self-determination.

So, if traditional philosophy doesn't perish through circumstances from the outside but through itself then this kind of self-explanation is absurd.

Traditional philosophy destroys its own myth. It discloses that every explanation it had offered and still offers is, in fact, not a true explanation. This further concludes that everything is different from how philosophy portrayed it and also that philosophy is different from what it wanted to be through self-determination. It further explains that the relationship between theory and practice is also different from our previous assumptions. With that Adorno introduces a way of thought which we have come to know as the "new order of pictures." The new order solves the "puzzle" of a philosophical understanding that leaves reality (and philosophy itself) undefined in important areas.

This kind of philosophy, according to Adorno—quoting Nietzsche—should be pushed while it is falling. This push aims at the destruction of the classic dichotomies of nature and history, subject and object, form and contents; as a theory of cognition they form the foundation of philosophy. The extremes of these dichotomies must be proven invalid in the course of a new order; which means it must be proven that there is only a terminological separation of things which actually form unities.

Yet, if nature and history, for example, originally form a unity, and if they are not two different things as the terminological "details" suggest, then it still does not conclude that natural history (namely this unity) become in fact a reality in itself. Because nature and history are separate things in the terminology of science and philosophy, it indicates that natural history is defined by nonidentity. Natural history cannot be itself when man exploits and suppresses nature and his fellow human beings; when everything is experienced and organized in terms of control.

The craft of control, which combines with the dominant abstract principle of barter in Economics, is also responsible, in the area of thought, for the non-identity of natural history. This nonidentity is seen in the separation of nature and history.

Similar considerations are possible regarding the relationship of subject and object, form and contents. Adorno accuses the phenomenological theory of cognition with losing sight of reality by reducing reality in the same way it was added to consciousness and that this kind of reality is not reality itself. The particular knowledge structure is made absolute; the contents of perception and the process of thought are taken as the "subject matter." Reality becomes valid if it passes the screening process of perception and fits into the laws of thought. This also means that an "order" of beings is hypostatized: the more important something is for thought (in the course of self-evaluation) the higher is its value. Judgement, valid for the process of thought when it is portraying truth, is projected onto the existing: the more static, the better. To measure everything existing with the standards of thought is contradictory, according to Adorno, because everything is then forced to be different from what it really is.

Adorno differentiates in this regard between two kinds of contradiction. The first kind of contradiction is found with Hegel. Hegel's dialectics contain the concept of absolute knowledge; however, this claim in itself will contradict itself and immanently reveal its untenability. Yet, this contradiction is by no means only philosophically immanent. It also points beyond philosophy to the antagonisms within society. Beside philosophical moments other moments start playing a part where absolute knowledge itself reveals that it cannot meet the requirements of the absolute, which means, that it cannot be absolute if taken only by itself.

Admitting this points to some other requirement that is needed in order to define its own reality (if this is in principle still possible). The conclusion is that thought cannot at all define the absolute from within itself. Its own imaginations and standards are not sufficient. Thought progressed because it believed it was able to draw standards for the absolute from itself and thus to produce it autonomically—now we see that it cannot meet this self requirement and the demand for self-generation.

Adorno establishes another kind of contradiction with the "positive philosophers" who do not develop an antithesis, as did Hegel. Husserl also falls under this category. Adorno assumes that Husserl wants to restore this *prima philosophia*; he believes that the spontaneous thought process is the only origin of concepts. This separates the subject that thinks reality from the object which is imaginary reality. Concepts are expression of this separation and thus of the non-identity of subject and object. Hegel still indicates this moment of non-identity in his idea of the absolute, yet he does it in an abstract way. However, Husserl denies the moment of non-identity completely because, in his view, only the factually existing is real. That is *mirabili dictu* according to Adorno; it is too little because the non-being is quite a part of reality—not in a mystifying way but exactly as non-identity: not many things can be themselves; terminology separates nature and history, subject and object, form and contents.

This new order is not a static new hierarchy which supersedes the old one but rather a process of continual softening of rigid images. This process is not controlled by an order of thought or by a supposed order of the cosmos. It cannot be measured at all without the existence of thought and reality as a unity.

According to Adorno, the new order of pictures should be understood as an interplay among the totality of existing things. No element should be given priority over other elements, or exercise control over them. The existing has neither priority over the synergy of existing and non-existing, nor over an entity which is simultaneously seen as identity and non-identity. Adorno develops this equality among nature, history and thought in the above sense where the three moments mutually define each other. These ideas must be understood as an "antithesis" to Husserl's phenomenology in so far Husserl had tried to prove that thought is the all dominant moment; dominant in regard to definition but also as the moment that controls reality. This suggests that the mind renders everything that is not equal to it to the control by the method (which had been detached from the subjects of cognition) so it can be unrestrictedly applied.

The method to understand the unknown, which only exists to understand the unknown, must always use force to mold that which
is different into its own image. . . Yet this method, constituted to
separate itself from its subject, appears in society as the separation of intellectual work and physical labor. In the process of work
common methodological procedures are the result of specializa-
tion, but the mind which is confined to special functions, misun-
derstands itself in its privileged way as the absolute.[20]

Philosophy can obscure the socially superior value of thought
and the associated practice of control, and thus stabilize itself so-
ciopolitically, when it doesn't make clear that concepts mediate
between socially and scientifically separated areas such as nature and history, sociology and psychology, subject and object;
and if and when it doesn't show simultaneously that this separation is wrong. Philosophy acts "restoratively" when it lifts the
sphere of concepts above everything and thus, simultaneously,
realizes and legitimizes the dominance of thought. This criticism
leads Adorno to a programmatic conclusion: "To perform dialectics in a concrete way."[21]

Adorno implements a program to define the relation between
thought and reality. The subject is that which reality thinks, and
the object is what is thought by the subject; both are only super-
ficially different from one another. Thinking means to think something concrete; therefore thought is defined through something
concrete. On the other hand, the "something" has always been
fictitious, only comprehensible in thoughts. The unity that comes
thus into focus should not be understood as absolute identity because the unity is, as shown, only a certain constellation of related thoughts with reality under "present" circumstances and which
could be different again under different circumstances. The in-
stance of the possibility-to-be-different means a permanently ongoing non-identity of the existing with itself. One can even say
that the literal affirmation that something had reached its identity, indicates its destruction. Then it can no longer be different
from what it is and therefore it is indifferent, dead—no longer

master of its own fate but dominated by something alien (assuming that it wants to live, even in the trap of self-sacrifice).

Tradition contains the characteristics of "establishing," of "making something stable" because a certain kind of self-preservation (that of the bourgeois consciousness) requires the exercise of control. Control stabilizes the circumstances and makes the world (physically and socially) transparent and controllable. But to control the world also strikes back at the one who is in control—he also "stabilizes" himself, suppresses the moment of change, of losing himself in indulgence, as it is shown in the *Dialectic of Enlightenment*. Adorno sees the beginnings of this development in the forming of mythology. Prehistoric man had tamed nature and its forces because he had found explanations which forced the unpredictable into a firm pattern of explanations—"already myth is enlightenment, and enlightenment returns to mythology"[22] because "with increasing demythologizing the philosophical concept becomes more metaphysical and also more mystical."[23] Adorno views the whole western tradition as a culture in which this mythologizing and stabilizing has succeeded. Adorno also defined his own philosophical program as "demythologization" but in the sense of a dialectical reconstruction of what had been lost in myth and the Enlightenment—namely, accepting the possibility-to-be-different, the negativity of the existing and of our judgements. This again exceeds traditional philosophical perceptions of thought since they principally can't bring the negativity into the open.

However, when traditional philosophy carries its theory of cognition to extremes something becomes visible that, in a sense, could be called "true."

> A theory of cognition is true in so far as it acknowledges its own dispositions as impossible and lets itself drift every step in the insufficiency of the subject. However, traditional philosophy is untrue in its pretension that it has succeeded, and that its constructions and aporetical concepts have ever complied with simple facts.[24]

Traditional philosophy is further "untrue" when it portrays its basic contradiction as merely temporary and when it believes that a correction of its methods would solve the problem. To portray its inadequacy as only a methodological question means, however, to deceive itself and others about the problematic relation between judgement and reality and to pretend that its own method is principally able to understand reality. This must be disputed, according to Adorno. The traditional method alienates when it "affirms," since it grasps something that cannot be retained as reality, which is not "established" and does not stand still. There is no firm correlation between judgements.

Adorno calls traditional philosophy simultaneously "true" and "untrue," which is not at all a contradiction born of ignorance—as analytically oriented philosophers like to claim—but rather a reference to the factual position of traditional philosophy whose inconsequence can hardly be blamed on the critics although they can be explored sociopsychologically. (Adorno reminds us of the students of the Sixties who are likely to be blamed for those scandalous circumstances that they had dared to criticize.) The point is that traditional philosophy falsely posits reality as true and negatively judges the possibility to be proven wrong as non-philosophical because it accepts only criticism that proceeds from its own preconditions of perception and method of thought. Its self-understanding becomes imperative and determines only methodologically what must be reality and what not.

In this way everything that is understood as non-identity and as being-different no longer falls into the area of philosophical reflection. The dynamic changes of reality are no longer taken into account because the predetermined categorical claims of the method together with the eternal perception of truth accept only the "always-remaining-the-same-in-itself" as possible truth. Adorno calls this self-hypostatizing of the method the "ontologizing" of philosophy wherein it has separated itself from the possibility to recognize reality, and from its own limits.

Philosophy must therefore once again bring its own non-identity to bear. This requires, as Adorno calls it, "metacriticism." This term does not imply a new, further differentiated methodological criticism but rather that philosophy must concentrate on what has been, up to now, philosophically unworthy, and on the (traditionally understood) peripherally philosophical subject, namely social life.

> Real life in society is the center of the logical constructs themselves and not something that has been smuggled into philosophy sociologically or by definition.[25]

As long as this social life is characterized by conflicts of interest and by an ideology with the function to disguise itself, philosophy cannot concentrate, even methodologically, on the requirements of non-contradiction. Something that is contradictory in reality cannot be portrayed free of contradiction. This does not conclude, however, that every statement is therefore permissible. Philosophy must rather see that reality can be itself and depart from contradiction. With that, philosophy would have freed itself from that "secret" contradiction which, up to now, it is subject to. One cannot conclude from this that philosophy would be made indifferent in this absolute identity. But it could then accomplish what it had intended to—the true portrayal of the existing—according to the reciprocity of the moments and not in the indifferent snapshots of the theory of cognition.

This program also determines Adorno's review of the inner dynamics of the development of philosophy. He points out an analogy with music which had [historically] "served" as entertainment for the rich yet nevertheless overcame itself in its development. Thus, even an invalid theory of cognition will contain concepts that pursue its transformation from the inside. The measure of philosophical criticism is here the downfall of existing pretensions. "When the period of interpreting the world has gone and when the world must be changed," as Adorno says in pointing at Marx, "then philosophy bids farewell, and in so doing the concepts come to a standstill and become pictures"[26] while philosophy and criticism become likewise superfluous.

3

THE ENLIGHTENMENT DEVOURS ITS CHILDREN: THE *DIALECTIC* OF *ENLIGHTENMENT*

The *Dialectic of Enlightenment*, written and published by Adorno together with Horkheimer in 1947, debates the problem of the sorcerer's apprentice who can no longer control the forces he has conjured. The human being developed his rationality in his quest to master nature—now he turns his reason into an instrument of control. This "control" does not limit itself to the environment, nature and fellow human beings, but it also reaches back to its own nature. This gloomy view of cultural developments derives from an analysis of the situation during the last years of the Second World War and shows four aspects:

— reducing human reason to purely instrumentalist ways of thinking
— commercialization of culture
— increasing anti-semitism
— subsuming human interests to economic priorities
Although all four aspects are important for the understand-

ing of the horizon and the preconditions for Critical Theory and Adorno's philosophy, I will select here the first philosophical aspect in order to make the characteristics of the whole analysis clear. Adorno elaborates on this aspect in the first essay which also lent the book its title. The basic problems of *Dialectic of Enlightenment* can, for the time being, be summarized in three theses.

First: intention is the basis of our human actions and thoughts which inevitably turn into their opposite in our culture. Second: the order that is seemingly created by science and politics is only an illusion—behind it chaos is lurking. Third: crisis-ridden phenomena are not just sideline disturbances that a better scientific and political management could deal with. They are fundamental crises that have their deep roots in the handling of problems in an "instrumentalist" way that only focuses on "efficiency" and not on the problem of legitimizing our goals.

The existence of the above-mentioned problems becomes obvious under the following aspects:

— Individuality is threatened by downfall. The individual does not account for anything under fascism and neither, very generally, within economics or science regardless of the form of society.
— Solidarity is no longer an aspect or motive to unite with others to care about common interests. Fascism perverts perception and the reality of a "community."
— The "sciences" enforce these negative developments rather than fight against them.

Adorno and Horkheimer see the root of these problems in the human being who perceives and forms his relation to the environment, which means to nature and fellow human beings, under instrumentalist aspects. The instrumentalist attitude that defines everything in terms of means and ends, cause and effect, must be seen as a consequence of the ruthlessly egotistical pursuit of self-preservation (although no real "self" can be preserved according to the dictums of the Critical Theory).

This quest goes hand-in-hand with the development of anxiety toward the uncertainties of surrounding nature and the actions of other human beings. To suppress *angst* man creates myths for himself or, similar in its consequences, he produces an "explanation." The threatening circumstances become transparent in explanations; and the guidelines of our expectations and experiences correspond with them. Whatever serves as a stereotype explanation of natural events works to the inside as a disciplinary measure for one's own thought and experience. The price for this outer security is the sacrifice of a "total experience" or "the experience of the totality." Only this would be a self-experience, a constitution of the self. Yet, it cannot happen under present circumstances.

Horkheimer and Adorno illustrate the latter while putting self-preservation and self-loss into contrast.[27] In self-loss the human being experiences his "being-one" with the cosmos: he gains everything in losing his "limited" individuality. With this the individual perishes as an individual, following the alluring song of the sirens while he transgresses the limits of his individuality in boundless beauty and continues his existence as part of the world as a "whole." The anxiety towards self-loss—according to Horkheimer and Adorno—finds its consequent expression in the bourgeois consciousness that attempts to escape self-loss by spellbinding the boundless, the threat, with an "explanation." Therefore the possibility of experiencing the meaning of self-loss is suppressed. All thoughts and actions are targeted to self-preservation which implies that the relation between the self and the environment, as well as these single moments, must be understood under instrumentalist aspects. Instrumentalism in philosophy and science means the use of force directed not only to the outside—but also towards the inside. Rationality expresses the capability of the human being to exercise control in suitable ways.

But now we must picture self-loss as well as self-preservation as "natural" dimensions of experience. If self-preservation is then played off against self-loss, nature will turn against itself. Rationality, as a natural talent of the human being, suppresses the natural experience of self-loss for the sake of self-preservation.

The nature of man contains, therefore, moments that are in conflict with each other. This conflict is based on dynamics that become transparent as cultural development. To develop rationality as the "medium" of control appears to be the goal and value of culture. This contradiction is based on the understanding of dialectics that serves Horkheimer and Adorno as their philosophical model.

DIALECTICS

If the term "dialectics" is not limited only to a specific theory of thought (which would be absurd anyway), but expresses that our ways of thinking cannot be detached from what we call reality, then we can attribute this to Critical Theory in the following way: a development (whether, historical, political or cultural) is always an expression of the fact that two forces contradict each other. These two forces cannot exist without one another. They form a relationship that either helps both to exist, or neither of them.

To illustrate these things I'd like to point to Hegel's concretization of this theory as it is interpreted by Alexander Kojève. In *Phenomenology of Mind* Hegel shows—in the chapter on control and slavery — that the exercise of control is "in-itself" a logical and therefore also a realistic impossibility. (I cannot go into detail about the many shades of meaning of this parable.)

> If, as Hegel says, the human being is nothing but a desire that wants to be satisfied that other beings recognize its "exclusive" right for satisfaction, then it becomes clear that humans can only fully realize and express themselves (thus definitively satisfying themselves) when they find complete and general "recognition." On the other hand, if a majority of such desires seek general recognition then it becomes that his action, deriving from these desires (at least for the time being) can only be a "fight" over life and

death. It is a fight because everybody wants to subjugate the other, all others, through negating and destructive actions. It is a fight over life and death because the desire which corresponds with desire directed at itself exceeds the "biological" life form, so that this existence does not limit the action generated by the desire. In other words, the being risks his "biological life" to satisfy his "non-biological" desire. Hegel further says that a being that is incapable of risking its life to achieve goals that are not directly vital, or that cannot risk its life for "acknowledgement," to fight for "prestige," cannot be a true human being.

One has to assume that the fight [possibly] ends with "both" opponents surviving. As prerequisite for this one must "give way" to the other and submit oneself to the other, and mutually acknowledge the other. However one can also assume that the fight has a victor who is ready to give his last—victorious over those who cannot lift themselves (while facing death)—beyond their biological instincts of "self- preservation" or beyond their identity with their "animal" existence. To speak in Hegel's language: one must assume that there is a victor who becomes "master" of the defeated. Or, if you prefer, one who becomes "slave" of the victor. The difference existing between master and slave or, to be more precise, the "possibility" of a difference between "future" master and "future" slaves is the fourth and last premise of the *Phenomenology of Mind*.

The defeated subsumed his "human" desire for "recognition" beneath the "biological" desire to preserve life. This determines and reveals his inferiority—to himself and the victor. The victor had risked his life for a non-vital goal: this determines and reveals—to himself and the defeated—his superiority over biological life and therefore over the defeated. The difference between master and slave becomes thus "reality" in the existence of winner and loser and [the victory] is acknowledged by both.

Superiority of the master over nature finds its reason in the risk of life in the fight for prestige and it becomes reality through the factual "work" of the slave. The slave changes the "given existing" conditions of existence in a way that they conform with the master's requirements. Nature that had been changed through the slave's work serves now the master but without any need for the

master to return the favor. The slave-part of the active relation
to nature falls to the slave; while the master makes the slave serve
his purposes and forces him to work, he, the master also makes
nature serve his purposes and realizes his freedom in nature
(makes his freedom a "reality" in nature). The existence of the
master can therefore remain exclusively "belligerent": he fights
but he doesn't work. So far as the slave is concerned his existence
is limited to work which he performs to serve the master. He works
but he doesn't fight. And according to Hegel, only doings rendered
to serve somebody else are "work." In the strict meaning of the
word, doing that is human and humanizing. The being that does
something to satisfy its own instincts which are, as such, always
"natural" does not lift itself beyond nature; it remains a natural
being, an animal. But when I do something to satisfy an instinct
that is not "mine" I am then active for something that is, for me,
not instinct. I do something because of an "idea," because of a
non-biological "goal." And this metamorphosis of nature due to
a non-materialistic idea is "work" in the strict meaning of the word:
it is work that creates a non-natural, technical and humanized
world which is adjusted to the "human" desire of being a being
that has "proven" and shown in reality its superiority over nature through risking its life for the non- biological goal of recognition."[28]

Yet, if master and slave are from within themselves and in
regard to one another conceptually contradictory and realistically
impossible, then all circumstances that are expressions of control are logically impossible and cannot be upheld. Then it is valid
to say that whenever such circumstances exist everything will
obviously appear different from its own true reality. However,
this observation requires that those circumstances will be
abolished.

Marx determines dialectics in a quite similar way. When Marx
states that capital and hired labor [work for wages] are contradictory then he shows not only the contradiction in their relation
but also that capital and work-for-wages are contradictory in
themselves.

Summarizing, we can say that a dialectical view portrays reality as a development that is based on two conflicting moments. These two moments are each in an ongoing conflict in so far as they bear the contradiction to the other in themselves and contradict one another. This conflict exists in theory as well as in reality. It causes their relation and also their appearance to be different from what they really are. This different appearance cannot be eliminated through changing the controlling circumstances between both moments but only through banishing the circumstances altogether.

With Hegel and Marx the question remains open whether one of the moments might nevertheless finally get the upper hand. Horkheimer and Adorno, however, proceed from their belief that the dialectic moment will come to a standstill. The conflicting moments of subject and object, nature and history, form and content remain existing in fluctuation. True, the circumstances, the "pictures" change and with them also the moments of this fluctuation, but the "Critical Theorist" doesn't believe in a total metamorphosis. The negative remains a constituting moment of the fluctuation and it prevents everything from becoming "itself"—totally identical to itself. It even prevents us from possibly imagining it.

In *Dialectic of Enlightenment* Horkheimer and Adorno pursue the question how far traditional philosophy and social reality are dialectically related. Philosophy does indeed claim to lead the action, to be ethical-practical in the form of methodological criticism, and technical-practical in the theory of cognition. Philosophy appears, therefore, as a seigniorial moment in relation to practice.

It is not difficult to guess that Horkheimer and Adorno view this seigniorial role of philosophy with great skepticism. The control of rationality which is so prominently portrayed in philosophy points itself to the inadequacy of this control because it is enforced through the absolutizing of its own standards. This places the development of method above the development of "reasonable" practice that leads to the instrumentalizing of our perception, to the absolutizing of the aspect of affectivity and thus to the oppression of the "natural" empirical dimension. It is revealing in this context how the "Critical Theorist" views the phenomenon of the Enlightenment.

THE ENLIGHTENMENT

In *Dialectic of Enlightenment* Horkheimer and Adorno proceed from their view that the sciences contributed to the improvement of life until the 18th century. Developing rational explanations led to an increased control over natural events and thus to improved tools and production. In the 18th century the human being distanced himself from the mythological imaginings which he had nurtured about society. To contribute towards that is the goal of Enlightenment philosophy. It makes clear that man should not judge social and political circumstances based on uncritically adopted tradition nor under the control of clerical authority but rather only based on personally formed judgements. This will guarantee that society (and also nature) can be controlled and can thus be submitted to rational and justifiable goals.[29]

The rationality of explanations and the controllability of social processes are seen in a fundamental context—one can almost say: in an "identity." This conception, represented by the philosophy of the Enlightenment, is also proof for Horkheimer and Adorno and their thesis about "explanations" (in contrast to common understandings of science), which posits that explanations were never merely "descriptions" that left what is being described untouched. The explanation already implies that the explained is subject to influence. This means that power is exercised in the form of a dissociated description that disguises the factual use of power.

It is a fact that Enlightenment philosophy would like to make its contribution to abolish the control of humans over humans and it indeed does it—with the best intentions—in helping to organize bourgeois society. Yet, at the same time—as Horkheimer and Adorno believe—it creates a new tyranny: man is forced to think and act rationally. This mandate of the Enlightenment requires that the measure of rationality becomes a universally valid standard. Everything is defined and treated in terms of instrumental effectiveness and controllability. However, if man thinks, experiences and treats nature in terms of controllability, then the ways in which he thinks about, experiences and treats himself must also be considered.

We must remember that not only the world and man are categorized as "natural" (assuming they exist physically), but that man's capability to reason is also seen as a natural ability. We must believe then that nature is here played off against nature. However, our discussion about dialectics has shown that a conflict of this kind provides a balance of control which appears, at first glance, relatively stable; yet we know that such a relation cannot last, neither in its definition nor in reality.

Such a relation between man and nature may cause man to occasionally and temporarily use force against himself and his fellow men. This is exactly designed into the philosophy of the Enlightenment. The control of rationality that man uses over nature, he turns against other human beings. Man does not understand his own existence and form of life in the sense of "good practice" but rather in terms of smooth functioning where the goal of this functioning will exhaust itself in precisely these functions. Control over external nature turns into control over the internal (human) nature. Its a case of self-slavery because man plays off the two natural forces which define him as human being. These facts are again reflected in society as the oppression of human beings by human beings.

These conflicting elements must be reconciled with each other in the course of a dialectic movement—not through an inversion of the power balance but through the elimination of the conflict itself. This requires that we eliminate the fixity of our thinking and standards. Myth and rational explanations determine the relation between man and nature, as well as man and his fellow men. A definition of this kind is obviously always necessarily produced from an abstract fixed-point, such as the prejudiced opinion about the value of a certain method. One must prove, on the contrary, that such a relation must always be understood from the inside. This alone produces the prerequisite [notion] that we don't define everything in terms of control. The use of external standards leads to totalitarianism, as in the case of an enlightenment which measures everything with the standards of rationality.

Horkheimer and Adorno see totalitarianism originate in the fear [*angst*] that befalls man when he realizes that he is, first and last, at the mercy of nature. *Angst* urges man towards tyranny over external nature. The successful constitution of this control seduces him to "acknowledge power as the principle of all relations."[30] This unfortunate dialectic of the Enlightenment, however, causes the opposite of its original intentions. The exercise of control turns everything into its opposite and leaves nothing as it really is. Man uses rationality to control nature out of fear of nature but he falls back into nature. He uses his natural ability to rationalize as an instrument against his own nature but this will only trigger an escalation of *angst* and oppression.

4

CRITICISM OF POSITIVISM

Meanwhile the dispute being propagated about the "correct" method in the social sciences found its first climax at the 1961 conference of the German Society of Sociology in Tübingen.[31]

The discussion took place between representatives of a strictly empirical model of social sciences—represented by philosophers such as Hans Albert and Karl A. Popper—and the supporters of a critical social science that also reflects its function in society, as required by Adorno and Horkheimer. The empiricists took the view that sociology must limit itself to the collection of data; basically, sociology should categorize appearing [social] aspects with the help of specific terminological schemata. A classic example for the latter is Talcott Parsons's structural-functionalist method.

Social phenomena can be categorized with the help of dichotomous terminological pairs, but they neither help to explain nor to understand these phenomena. However, it seems that this ordering is already the explanation.[32] This apparent aspect reveals what Adorno calls the "predominance of terms" or the "predominance of terminological order," and which he criticizes as such. The "thought" determines reality. But, methodological thinking is blind in regard to certain aspects because it only sees what can be understood within the framework of terminological definitions. The structure of our conceptual order is assumed to be identical with the structure of things or their relations. Adorno accuses the empiricists and positivists of relying on experiences that have already been pre-screened by their conceptual order. The positivists don't admit that their experiences have already been theoretically pre-structured.

In addition, Adorno criticizes that this method proceeds unreflectedly from its claim that it could improve the [social] situation from within and by itself. Adorno believes that this claim is totally unfounded. The empirical method that is allegedly without prejudice, contributes to the manifestation of the existing balance of power regarding man and nature, and also regarding the relation between man and his fellow-men. Applying the empirical method [to social realities] is basically nothing else but a specific use of the model of rationality.

Thus Adorno denies that empirical social sciences contribute or are able to contribute to the humanization of our living conditions. The old European ideal of order and progress, as it was formulated by the founder of Positivism, Auguste Comte, is still at work; carried to extremes one can say that progress equals, in this context, a respectively more rigid order because it enhances and facilitates the controllability of human beings. According to Adorno, it was the extraordinarily rapid progress in the natural sciences at the beginning of the century that had seduced social sciences to this one-sidedness. The real reason for it, however, lies with a specific philosophical understanding of rationality, as we have shown.

This philosophical conception advances the opinion that order is a matter of mind or method. The method is given priority in so far as it is completely a product of thought and thus depends on thought and thought alone. The process of thought produces and controls itself in the method; it categorizes and stimulates technical and social practice with the help of ideals that are taken from the conception of logical consistency and (static) uniformity.

This priority of the method implies a separation of method and subject. The subject shows itself only so far as it permits or doesn't permit successful action. The success of the action determines, therefore, the truth contents of the theory, while we understand success only under its instrumentalist aspects, which means in terms of problem solving. Adorno doesn't completely condemn this view but it is very limited in the development of existing circumstances which will, as many believe, lead to a catastrophe if we don't reconsider the total goals of human actions. What is the meaning of "progress," of "order," if we don't constantly rethink and redefine these terms regarding good practice? The meaning of "good practice" should not be defined only instrumentally as the capacity for problem solving, let alone as [simply] a matter of logical consistency or differentiating measures of a scientific method.

The fact that the social sciences (and also natural sciences) persistently eliminate questions from their scope as non-scientific questions (namely questions about the legitimate use of technologies) and whether everything that can be performed may and must be performed. With regard to this, Adorno points to the sciences which are blind toward their central questioning, namely the question of their social effectiveness. This blindness is an expression of a dichotomous separation of moments that basically form a singularity but disintegrate practico-politically in the face of an instrumentalist solution and moral legitimation. This disintegration is consistently accompanied by the perception of science's "objectivity." The further science removes itself from questions of justification, the more objective and, therefore, scientific is the perception of our knowledge.

Adorno, however, believes that social reality cannot be viewed independently from a "scientific" point of view. We must understand that more and more areas of our society (schools, mass media, etc.) are increasingly affected by sciences, and that our society increasingly orientates the picture which it has formed of itself on the model of scientific order. This model has a hierar-

chical structure through and through. The method, in its abstract
and thus universal triviality, has priority over every particular
single appearance. Empty generalities always rank above the (specifically defined) individual statement. This hierarchy is by no means as "objective" as is pretended; it is rather subjective to the
degree where science itself speaks in derogatory terms of the
"merely subjective." The self-hypostatizing of the method characterizes the so-called objectivity.

This reveals itself very clearly where social science encounters the phenomenon of hierarchical social divisions. Social
sciences accept without criticism that individuals experience social differences in income, status and prestige as given social reality, and they [social sciences] merely describe the social experience
of individuals in terms of these "orderly" differences. Yet, with
that, social sciences proceed from a derived phenomenon instead
of an original one since the differences in income, status and prestige stem from an existing class relation which disguises [the fact]
that the experience of differences is not natural. Social sciences
thus busy themselves with superficial phenomena behind which
the social reality of class differences disappears. Adorno also criticizes that social sciences proclaim something as public opinion
which is basically only the statistical mean of public opinion polls.
Furthermore, the usefulness of the polls becomes problematic,
especially the significance of the opinions that deviate from statistical means. At those times, when we radically level all personal
opinions, statistical means are of no value whatsoever.

Consequently, social sciences should first of all reconstruct
the original unity of method and (the examined) subject and then
turn to answering specific questions. A reconstruction of that kind
should prove that neither method nor fixed reality deserves priority, nor is the mediation between method and reality of an ontological nature.

To demand that the investigating method and the examined
subject form one unit expresses, therefore, that social reality does
not only consist of traditional legalisms and other mechanisms

of distribution and production but very basically of views that human beings have about society. These views cannot be seen atomistically as private [views] but rather as something that has been formed through communication. They've been produced by context-dependent and [process-like] information from different conceptions and refer to that social reality whose contradictory basic characteristics we have already proven.

Adorno suggests that the social sciences exclude this social contradiction from examined conceptions since the conceptual framework of the social sciences sets them aside for being inconsistent. In this way we lose the possibility to see the fundamental contradiction in society and to understand social phenomena which are based on it. Although Adorno draws very close to Marx in this respect, his theory still differs from Marx's argumentation. Adorno does not proceed from contradictions in the production process with its contrast between capitalist and worker, he rather proceeds from the process of exchange. Adorno believes that exchange as the fundamental commercial medium of bourgeois society changes even the most concrete relations into abstractions. Every need with regard to its contents must appear in the form of its exchange value before it can be satisfied. In agreement with that, Adorno says man experiences himself, his needs, capabilities and his fellow-men in the abstract forms of exchange. Abstraction as such becomes the medium and also the contents of all social and human relations. "Reducing human beings to agents and carriers of the exchange of goods establishes the control of human beings over human beings."[33]

The transformation of the particular and concrete into abstractions consequently leads to the control of the abstract over the concrete as empty methods gain control over the examined subjects due to their "universal validity." The control of man is a logical consequence of the control of the abstract because now generalities rank above the single, individual subject. "The abstraction of the exchange value is *a priori* linked to the control of the common over the singular, of society over its coerced members."[34] This aspect of universality as something absolute is perceived by Adorno as ontologizing contradictions which were produced by society, and also the unjustifiable determination that the common is given priority over the individual.

In fighting this development Adorno does not erect a new abstract principle against the old one, and neither does he project a Utopia. Like Marx, Adorno wants to bring the existing circumstances into the open by confronting them through themselves. A new order of the "pictures," a new perspective of the relation between the common and the particular proves the "falseness" of the circumstances. This will consequently lead to the understanding of the role which the procedure of abstraction plays in science and philosophy. Both these areas of abstraction are complementary to each other; both express that man no longer controls his circumstances and actions. The abstract principle likewise controls everybody and reduces everybody to a pre-written character role and to [the exercise of] an instrumentalist function—capitalists and workers alike.

However, the abstract principle of exchange disguises conflicting interests. The difference between things that are basically non-equivalent (intrinsic value and value of exchange) disappears in abstraction. Such circumstances can only be illuminated in the form of criticism. Philosophy's epoch as the portrayer of truth is over since the ways in which subjects and their relations appear no longer agree with what they are based on. Traditional philosophy still believed it could proceed from the assumption that differences between theory and reality could be eliminated through correcting or differentiating the method. A "fact" derived from a basic agreement between a judgement and what had been judged. Thus philosophy could develop in the form of grand systems, these systems following the idea that one could force reality to appear in its true form if one succeeded in producing a comprehensive system of opinions with their basic layout and derivates. Such a system would necessarily reveal how the difference of judgement (meaning thinking) and what was judged could be suspended in the system of thought itself and with that one would have solved the classic problem of truth.[35]

If, however, reality has become inconsistent within itself, if human beings experience themselves and others only in terms of abstract exchange and if they no longer control their actions and thoughts, then the theory cannot be what it has been defined as (from within itself): the portrayal of truth. If society has become untrue and false, this theory which is fundamentally the theory of society, can no longer portray the truth. But, if this theory portrays society as it is (and that is its task), it will portray the untrue and false. Yet, theory can only justify the above in showing the existing to be untrue and false, which means when it articulates itself as criticism. But even as theory, criticism remains linked to social circumstances because the measure for correct criticism lies in the discrepancy within the real.

What this change of grand theory into criticism implies for philosophy is equally valid for social science. It [social science] must also develop as criticism and must not jump from one partial analysis to another claiming performance of a systematic portrayal. In this respect, philosophy and social science could unite. "The idea of scientific truth cannot be separated from the truth of a true society."[36]

5

WHAT DOES ADORNO CALL MATERIALISTIC, HISTORICAL AND DIALECTICAL?

Adorno explicitly characterizes his thinking as materialistic and dialectical. There is no doubt that it is also justified to call it historical. With this, three of the most important aspects of dialectical philosophy are united. Nevertheless, Adorno's philosophy has been criticized time and again on the grounds that it cannot, justifiably, be called materialistic and/or dialectical.

Who determines what can be called "materialistic" and "dialectical?" Is philosophy the wonderland of Alice in which Humpty Dumpty concludes that those who are in power determine the meaning of a word? It is common in philosophy to legitimize the use of terms through tradition. However, the exact meaning of a certain term in a specific tradition is also subject to reinterpretation (not to mention the fact that an entire philosophical perspective can itself be contested as to whether or not it belongs to a specific tradition).

The question whether a specific traditional term is justifiably used or not can probably only be answered when we agree on what philosophy represents for society. But that seems to be a rather hopeless undertaking. I therefore suggest—following the requirements of an introduction—that Adorno used the term "dialectical-materialist" so we can understand his philosophy as a consequence, or at least as a variation, of a certain tradition. I'd like to grant him (and others too) that the above can only be sanctioned if and when we refine these terms and portray the relation of philosophy and society philosophically, and when we stay away from purely terminological hair-splitting.

To categorize Adorno's philosophy from the outside poses the problem that "dialectical" must be understood [not only] in a sense of idealistic but also in a sense of materialistic dialectics. There are only a few [critics] who perceive Adorno as a real materialist, yet many see in him an idealist and accuse him of hiding his idealism behind a pseudo-materialism. This controversy cannot be simply solved since the idealists don't define themselves as what their opponents, the materialists, call idealism and vice versa. Here also, it is not the controversy about terms, I believe, but the relation between terms and reality that we must address. Regardless, the reference points in tradition are obvious: Hegel and Marx.

Despite all their differences, this is what they do have in common: both understand that dialectics develop a model of society and culture and thus generally a model of all forms of reproduction based on the conflict between opposing forces. Philosophy as criticism portrays itself as part of this development and thus becomes an immediate part of social practice. In this respect Adorno connects with Hegel and Marx. However, it seems to me, he significantly differs from Hegel and Marx because he sees no linearity in this movement, while they project history toward a goal, and with that, toward an end. In Adorno's understanding the movement wanders back and forth between two or more extremes. Reality, in each case, is a special constellation of different elements that keep themselves in motion but without a goal.

There are changing constellations in the relation of subject and object, nature and history, science and society. None is "more true" than another. In each case, one can only find out what constitutes their difference. There is no Archimedes' point from which the whole [picture] could be developed. This change of dialectical perspectives is probably linked to Adorno's understanding of the negative, in contrast to Hegel and Marx. They see the negative as a necessary component of history and, principally, of any movement and development. But, since they believe in an end to history (Hegel sees the dispersal of bourgeois society into the state, Marx sees the empire of freedom) they also see the suspension of negativity (as negation of the negation) at some point, which means that it will finally be eliminated.

In contrast, Adorno believes in the existence of the negative as long as something exists at all. He cannot imagine that there could be a real totality one day, that everything could ever be as it is supposed to be and that it will ever reach a quiet end. In other words: all that is thought can never become social reality, and reality can never be identical with thought. The history of the exercise of power cannot be turned back. Even the imagined thought that it could be different is a mere hope that only demonstrates the misery of the existing situation. In so far as man has won his fight for self-preservation against external nature, he has also split himself into a first (natural) and second (social) nature, and thus he has forever gambled away the possibility to find his oneness with himself as nature. Lost identity cannot be brought back, just as Orpheus could never save Eurydice from the realm of the dead.

THE MATERIALISTIC MOMENT

To accuse Adorno of idealism finds its base especially in his belief that cultural phenomena strongly influence historical developments. The critics contend—more or less justly—a specific view of Marx according to which only the process of production has a causal influence on historical development and all other social phenomena must be seen as a consequences of the production process.

It is correct that Adorno grants great importance to intellectual activities, such as art. He believes that social reality consists fundamentally of just these activities and that they characterize the picture of reality. However, I have tried to point out that Adorno does not believe that these activities have any factually determining effect, like his opponents assume. Adorno sees social life reproducing itself in the back-and-forth struggle of man—who himself is also nature—with nature, as a biological-natural struggle to produce a human, rational and social nature. None of these components can claim to be an actual origin. This should really become obvious in Adorno's criticism of traditional philosophy. He accuses traditional philosophy of having degenerated into a mere theory of cognition which means that it has created its own world (its own process of cognition) instead of dealing with social circumstances as a whole.

Adorno's materialism does not comply with Marx in making organized work the starting-point of social developments and, with that, the basis of his theory. Yet, it does make sense to talk about Adorno's materialism. His criticism of traditional philosophy as a [mere] theory of cognition reveals that this view of reality cannot be seen under "materialistic" aspects as having priority, [and it also reveals] that he does not believe that social events and developments were directly influenced by intellectual activities. The fluctuation, mentioned by Adorno, between the historic-socially separated moments (subject/object and nature/history) should make clear that the classic terminological separation of idealism and materialism is outdated. It is no longer important to observe how those opposites are played off against one another. It is rather important to see that familiar antitheses form basically a singularity, although this singularity cannot be perceived as being totally identical with itself.

When we say that Adorno's philosophy can be called materialistic, we do so justly because his view of science and philosophy is as little "idealistic" as his understanding of the materialistic basis of society is purely "economic." Adorno intends to show that the traditional separations of theory and reality have lost their purpose. In its idealism, theory has become—even in its "falseness" as a theory of cognition—a materialistic force since it perpetuates the existing balance of power. Likewise, materialism, in the form of an economic conception of values, has become the *leitmotif* that controls everything. In a social reality in which the "idealistic" and the "materialistic" exchange roles, only the materialist theory can produce from within itself the basic prerequisites that everything can become again (or for the first time) what it should be. In doing so it is also quite important to reveal that playing off "first" nature against "second" nature is contradictory and would grant criticism a (materialistic) *fundamentum in re*. With that the picture of a theory that has distanced itself from practice [reality] has disappeared. To eliminate the distance between theory and practice expresses itself in the disappearance of the control that man has over man.

Adorno's philosophy is propelled by establishing that the existing circumstances are perceived by man differently from what they really are. For this Adorno finds the most proof in the fact that human beings experience and think about themselves, others and their social relations in terms of abstractions which are carried to extremes in the exchange of goods. In this respect, Adorno's philosophy also has a materialistic basis. It becomes clear that social criticism is simultaneously criticism of philosophy as a theory of cognition, and that criticism of the theory of cognition is simultaneously, and in the same regard, criticism of the existing social circumstances.

THE HISTORICAL MOMENT

The historical perspective has already become clear in the way Adorno portrayed the relation of nature and history. Adorno tries to prove that our concepts as well as everything we experience in reality is of an historic nature. The concepts we use are historically imprinted; these include terms we use to express that something is unchangeable. Adorno shows that the perception of immutability is connected with abstract thinking in the way it effects society and establishes control. The abstraction of exchange values is analogous to abstract thinking in science and philosophy. The concept of eternally valid truth uses standards that our mind defined for itself. Yet, this conceals that the values we view as "eternally valid" are themselves expression of a certain interest, the interest of exercising control. This conception certainly has a historic character since it always materializes under historically concrete conditions.

The use of immutable concepts such as "nature" isolates, says Adorno, the scientific, philosophical and practico-political moment from the grand picture of existence. But this isolation is mere artifice since it contradicts the characteristics of all existing things — to be historical. These characteristics reveal themselves in everything existing that is given to our consciousness. If consciousness itself is of an historical nature then everything else is likewise of an historic nature. (If the existing does not emerge, which means if it is not given to consciousness, then it is pointless to talk about its existence. We neither know whether it exists, nor how it exists.)

For Adorno, the concept "nature" and its correlates are also historically determined. The separation of nature and its immutable laws on the one hand, and the changeable aspects of history on the other hand, cannot be upheld. The separation of the changing and the immutable does not happen between nature and history but through nature itself.

The analogous is valid for history. History can be changed

but it also has an immutable core. For example, the fact that human beings exercise control over human beings cannot be denied. Yet how it is historically dealt with is an open question, even though Adorno himself is not very optimistic in this regard. He believes that under the existing conditions, history cannot be defined from within so therefore it cannot be the result of human actions. History cannot be influenced by human rational planning—it emerges in turns of war and peace and with more or less severe economic crises which appear to be an inevitable part of nature.

There is a correlation between the fact that man experiences history as something occurring outside of his scope of influence, and history in its reality. Conformity alone between history, as humans understand it, and history, as it really is, cannot be the only criterion for the truth of ideas as portrayed by traditional philosophy. What history could be in reality, does not find justness unless man shapes it consciously. History, and also the understanding of history as it is, are falsified. Subsequently, the accord between the concept and its correlate is also false. The correction of this distortion, the new order of fixated "pictures," will show that history is through and through "natural" in the sense that the new pictures will eliminate the existing separation between the changing and the immutable.

To avoid a common misunderstanding I'd like to point out that the above does not imply that nature and history become totally identical. The unity of nature and history is characterized through its ability to change. Negativity remains the decisive moment for the existing as well as for our understanding of it. It is this negativity, however, that determines the course of the unity between nature, history and our consciousness. Yet, history is not a linear development or teleology but a constantly renewed configuration of "pictures."

THE DIALECTICAL MOMENT

The dialectical moment of Adorno's philosophy reveals, first of all, that he doesn't perceive the existing reality as a closed, completely identical unity but as a conflict between opposing forces. This conflict separates conceptually what is in reality one: subject and object, nature and history, contents and form, individual and society, thought and reality. Adorno defines these opposing moments as forms of appearance and fact which complement each other. The one cannot exist without the other. Their conceptual separation is artificial. Both sides are "equally original" and likewise "effective."

Adorno's concept of equal opposites clearly differs from Marx's dialectical conception. As we have explained, Marx considers one of the two opposing moments superior to the other. In the relation of capital and labor the latter is the source on which capital feeds like a parasite. This false appearance which is simultaneously also reality, suggests that capital is the stronger element while, in fact, it is the dependent one. The dialectical headway of historic reality is to correct the apparent superiority of capital and thus to eliminate the false understanding of the power balance between capital and labor.

Adorno does not in principle grant any superiority to one or the other moment of a dialectical relation. To imagine that one of these elements would be more essential or more effective than the other would indicate for Adorno that something is wrong in so far as we would still be thinking in terms of control. True reality reveals itself in the fact that there is no control and that a difference in power does not, therefore, factually exist. Adorno doesn't think in terms of inferiority or superiority regarding these opposing moments; he rather thinks in terms of the ability to transform and change or not to change. He accuses traditional philosophy and science of dichotomizing reality into a contrast of change and immutability thus creating the prerequisites for everything to conform with the ideal of immutableness. The unchangeable, eternally valid, controls then the changeable.

Adorno opposes this theory in stating that everything is likewise changeable and unchangeable. The separation of changing
and not-changing does not happen between the moments of reality, and certainly not between the laws of thought and reality but
rather within everything itself; everything is constantly defined
by negativity within itself and in regard to consciousness. Revers-
ing the power balance cannot be a solution for society, rather
the elimination of the power balance is needed—however, that
is prevented through the dynamics of negativity once they are
set in motion. To explain the latter is the goal of *Negative
Dialectics*.

6

ADORNO'S *NEGATIVE DIALECTICS*

by Peter Schiefelbein

Negative Dialectics takes a central position in Adorno's thinking, mainly for two reasons: it represents the most differentiated, methodological reflection on his previous works and it is also the attempt to newly determine the relation of theory and practice far beyond what philosophy has yet produced—to "reach beyond the official separation of pure philosophy and facts or formal sciences."[1] The goal of this philosophical analysis is to prove the authenticity of a concrete philosophy that opposes all "approbated thinking." "Philosophy is not 'about' concrete things but rather is derived from them."[2]

METHODOLOGICAL REFLECTION

When *Negative Dialectics* was published in 1966 all of Adorno's [philosophical] work had already been offered. The subsequent methodological reflection within *Negative Dialectics*, which contradicts the traditional conception of philosophy, explains and justifies retrospectively the procedures of earlier works. "The procedure is not grounded but justified."[3]

This justification must be clearly kept apart from the term "proof" which belongs in the arena of idealistic thought. In methodological explanations of idealistic systems the objects can be completely ascribed to the identity of original and defining terms, while the methodology of *Negative Dialectics* reflects such an identity of subject and object as an illusion that conceals a situation of control which does not tolerate anything heterogenic to these terms. The identity of subject and object is produced by the fundamental functions of cognition [by the subject] and denies the qualitative definition of the objects that exists independently from the subject—in order to integrate it without contradiction into the rigid schematism of its terminology. The conception of *Negative Dialectics* evolves from the criticism of this deceptive identity.

> Once the author trusted his own intellectual impulses, he felt it to be his task to use the force of the subject to break through the deception of constitutive subjectivity; he didn't want to postpone this task any longer.[4]

This criticism starts with the conceptual mediation of subject and object. Adorno focuses on the non-identical, the conceptually undefined and unique which traditional philosophy ignores and suppresses as accidental and unimportant qualities. It is precisely these qualities of the object that should also be accessible—in the self-cognizance of philosophical thinking—to conceptual cognition: to break open the mechanism of conceptual control in recognizing its imperfection and lack of refinement. "The utopia of cognition would be to illuminate the conceptually undefined without setting concepts equal to it."[5] This thought inspires the idea of negative dialectics which want the dogmatic and rigid contents of concepts to fall apart.

> Their [negative dialectics] logic is one of deterioration: [the ruin] of the prearranged and prestructured design of concepts which is. first of all, directly confronted with the subject that is to be per-

ceived. Their identity with the subject is the untruth. With that the subjective pre-formation of the phenomenon moves ahead of the non-identical, ahead of the *individuum inefabile*. The essence of identical definitions corresponded with the ideal of traditional philosophy, its *a priori* structure and its archaic late derivative, ontology. Yet, this structure in an abstract definition has become, before any specific meaning, something negative in the most simple sense: the metamorphosis of force into thought. This negativity is still realistically in control. What could be different has not yet begun.[6]

Adorno tries to comply with this utopia of cognition in a new form of philosophical interpretation that exempts the concepts from being forced to a [certain] identity. The philosophical representation in which the linguistic contents of concepts and the expressiveness of the subject are stretched to extremes is an essential moment of the materialistic conception of negative dialectics which develop a completely new understanding of language regarding metaphysical tradition. According to Adorno this new understanding is already characterized in the literal sense of [the concept] dialectics.

Dialectic would be, in its literal sense, language as organon of thought [which] is the attempt to critically save the rhetorical moment: to approximate subject and expression to one another until they are indifferent. Dialectic dedicates to the power of thought that which seemed, historically, a flaw of thought—namely the connection of thought and language that cannot be shattered by anything.[7]

How emphatically Adorno understands the term "language" and [how emphatically] he separates it from traditional philosophy illustrates his judgement about Hegel's dialectics: "So far as Hegel remained an adept of traditional science, Hegel's dialectic was [dialectic] without language while the simple literal sense of the word 'dialectic' postulates language."[8]

In an essay entitled *These über die Sprache der Philosophen*[9] which was written in the early 1930's, Adorno formulated important language-philosophical thoughts which were essentially expanded and revised in *Negative Dialectics*. The thought from the theses: "All philosophical criticism is nowadays possible as criticism of language,"[10] is programmatic for *Negative Dialectics*. The possibility of materialistic dialectics depends on our efforts and success to re-provide dialectics—against their idealistic conceptual functions—with their essential linguistic moments.

> If the idealistic concept of dialectics does not bear experiences that are independent from the idealistic apparatus—contrary to Hegel's emphasis—philosophy has no other course than to lose its insight into content and it will restrict itself to the methodology of science, thus annulling itself.[11]

Hegel's dialectics largely lack the mimetic expressiveness— that has been pushed back further and further into the history of language—such that the concept has almost completely lost its original dialectical contents. Nevertheless, the mimetic moment is not completely to be lost from cognition.

> If this moment were totally extinct the subject could not possibly recognize the object, thus the [introduced] rationality would be irrational. However the mimetic moment itself blends together with the rational [moment] on the course of its secularization. This process can be summarized as differentiation.[12]

The differentiation of experience is linked to the original dialectical quality of language in which the mimetic modes of reactions of the individual subject and conceptual thinking come together as a unit. The mimetic conceptual moment of materialistic dialectics is, therefore, inalienable. The subject's mimetic moment of expression infiltrates the philosophical portrayal— which Adorno equates with the expression of language—and imparts to subjects a cognition of a higher grade of differentiation and objectivity than the mere application of rigid idealistic terminology would ever permit.

Its (philosophy's) integral moment of expression, non- conceptual mimetic, will only be objectified when performed as language.[13]

The individual subject articulates itself through mimetic impulses—far beyond the scientifically sanctioned contents of experience—which are dictated by the categorically composed unity of its transcendental subjectivity. This mimetic potential creates the possibility for a cognitive, unruled experience that tries to develop philosophical standards from an objective, conceptual definition of the experienced objects themselves rather than to dictate [the standards] to the objects as a subjective definition. Only this intellectual experience—that searches to understand its own intellectual structuralization of objects—can, although on a differentiated level of reflection, connect with the experience that the mimetic conception introduced to "primitive" men : to experience the transcendence of the single thing which is complexly connected with infinite nature as well as history and which, therefore, cannot be forced into a final identity with the concept.

What is, is more than it is. This 'more' is not forced on it but rather remains immanent to it as something that had been expelled from it . . . Communication with the other becomes clear in every singular moment that, in its existence, has been communicated through it.[14]

The concepts [inherent] in philosophical description permanently reflect the non-identity of concepts and subjects which then prevents subjects from being open in their own transcendency towards something else. This by itself reveals the untruth of the asserted identity of concept and subject. The untruth does not only exist as a forced synthesis and forced subsumption of the subject under the identity of the concept but also as an ideological disguise of historical definitions which are falsely introduced as natural. In the identity of concept and subject—in which truth is to be positive—subjects should [be permitted to] express their natural character; but in reality "even the trace of defining objects as such, their transcendency, is forcefully fixated to the immanence of the concept". The invariant concepts "transgress to ideology as soon as they are defined as transcendent."[15]

Philosophical portrayal that refuses all transcendent and factual determinations of truth—which lend language the claim for general acceptance and necessity—is, as performed by negative dialectics, determined by the paradox that it wants to express the nature of things without being "able" to express them. "The task of philosophical self-reflection is to unfold this paradox."[16] The "fragility" and the "undeciding [character]" of philosophical portrayal are found in the distance between idealistic and positivistic research techniques. Nevertheless, philosophical portrayal does not lack stringency: with the unbounded alienation of the subject to [the subject of] experience—which goes hand in hand with the most extreme efforts of conceptual definition—the movement of negative dialectics attempts to express the definition of subjects so linguistically differentiated that they escape the obligatory identity of classifying terminology—ones that attempt to define their nature — or, as Adorno writes regarding Benjamin's linguistic-philosophical term, [they escape] their "name."

> As one might think, this development in languages has its distant and vague origin in names which don't overinterpret the matter in categories at the price of losing their cognitive function... Idiosyncratic precision when selecting words as to whether they should [exactly] name the matter is not [at all] one of the least important reasons that presentation is very important to philosophy.[17]

Even with utmost linguistic precision, in the constellation of concepts that concentrate on the subject of cognition, one cannot put a name on things. However, the constellation of concepts is able to reveal some possibilities which have been buried by historical developments and which have been waiting to become reality as a condition of the truth in understanding a subject. This realization is not possible in the systematic self-containment of a specific theory of thought but only in "models" and "interventions" of philosophical thinking.[18]

What is waiting in [these possibilities] needs intervention in order to speak, with the perspective that every theory that has been applied to these phenomena will finally be satisfied in all these efforts that have been brought into it from the outside.[19]

Thought as well as subject find their final peace only in truth. To meet the possibility for truth, thought must become aware of its own imperfection. Adorno took on the immense task of criticizing philosophical tradition in order to be able to store it, with its truth content transformed, within the methodology of philosophical portrayal. "The positioning of thought towards happiness would be the negation of everything that is false."[20] This sentence might describe the intention that Adorno's self reflection upon philosophical thought is based upon.

THEORY AND PRACTICE

The possibility that philosophical theory will provide intellectual impulses that might create a reasonable social order, and a changed practice, is small under the present social circumstances of control and production. The reasons for the presently insignificant role of philosophy lie firstly, according to Adorno, in the inadequacy of philosophical reflection. Even Marxism (as the most elaborate historical-philosophical theory of revolutionary changes of human freedom overcoming social circumstances) fails to bring desired changes factually into reality because of the juvenile behavior of humans (which all political systems reinforce); and the incapability of humans to think of alternatives ways of living beyond the specific principles of their social realities; and the lack of desire to produce any changes in their social practice.

Freedom and reason—by no means the determining forces of our social order—have become an ideology that denies humans even the possibility of becoming aware of the limits and helplessness that has been forced upon them. Philosophy is co-responsible for this ideological disguise.

That freedom remains largely ideology; that humans are made helpless by the system and that they are incapable of determining their life and everything else from their reasoning; even that they are no longer capable of thinking about it without additional suffering; leads their protest into the wrong direction. They sarcastically prefer the worse over the pretension of [something] better. Contemporary philosophers contribute to all this. They already feel a unity with the rising order of the most powerful interests while they, like Hitler, play tragedians on a lonesome venture. The fact that humans act as if they are metaphysically homeless and are kept [perpetually] in the dark ideologically justifies the order that leads to despair and threatens human beings with physical destruction. The resonance of contemporary metaphysics is the agreement with that oppression that will be victorious—even in the West—due to its social potential; it had already been victorious in the East where the idea of demonstrated freedom has been twisted to unfreedom.[21]

Philosophy's indifference towards metaphysics leads to a betrayal of the Enlightenment. Philosophy, following the positivistic tendency of all other sciences, dismisses questions of metaphysics as irrelevant; thus it grants absolute metaphysical dignity to a social order which now appears to be the last and unchangeable legality. The "animalization" of social practice, which continues in an established social structure, without any awareness of other possibilities, is impossible without the neutralization of the human consciousness regarding the traditional metaphysical ideas of God, liberty, immortality and truth: they [all] relativize every social order, and question the purpose of existence. The possibility of a modifying theory depends on the possible conditions of metaphysical experience. Yet, the perception of metaphysical interests is prevented because humans "under the objective pressure of the bare necessities of life . . . [are consumed] by the humiliation of survival"[22]; the principle of self-preservation which has thus been given absolute priority forces them into it. The limitation of [our] consciousness which is based on the neutralization of metaphysical experiences implies simultaneously the loss of possible experiences of a practice that could be changed.

Materialistic denial forces the consciousness of the basic classes in exchange societies to limit itself to the possible interests of self-preservation. This constitution of society, which has not changed despite all cultural efforts and which threatens humans with their self-destruction—a possibility that one likes to neglect—found, up to now, only moments of philosophical consideration.

> Although aware of the facts, bourgeois society chooses total destruction, its objective potential, over the effort to reflect on the circumstances that are threatening its basic structure. The metaphysical interests of human beings also need the unimpaired understanding of their materialistic interests. As long as the latter remain uncertain, humans will live under the veil of Maya.[23]

The new aspect of Adorno's philosophy is the execution of this self-reflection which has been suppressed up to now. It consequently discusses the transition of metaphysics to materialism.

> In the course of history, materialism needs what was traditionally its direct counterpart: metaphysics. What the mind has once claimed to be of its own kind or what it had tried to construe is [now] headed for something that is [quite] unlike it: something that escapes its domain and reveals itself as something absolutely evil. The class of the living which is deprived of consciousness, is the scene of suffering that burns mercilessly everything that could console the mind and its objective representative, culture, in the camps [referring to the concentration camps of the fascists]. The process that has led metaphysics irresistibly into areas against which it had originally been created, has reached its point of escape. Ever since the young Hegel, philosophy has been unable to deny how much it has gotten involved with the questions of materialism.[24]

Adorno's thoughts focusing on what happened to humanity in Auschwitz have two roots: one stems from the author's shock and feelings of guilt as someone "who had accidentally escaped and should have been rightfully killed,"[25] guilt that would put in question his existence; the other reason [focusing on Auschwitz] was his understanding and knowing that suffering and indifference about the individual life had been brought to absolute extremes in Auschwitz. Philosophical self-reflection must deal with the unbearable experience of the industrial killing machine of Auschwitz in order to break with a cultural tradition whose failure has been, in Adorno's view, irrefutably proven in Auschwitz.

> If negative dialectics demand the self-reflection of thought then it clearly implies that thought, in order to be true, must also think against itself, at least nowadays. If thought doesn't measure itself against the most extreme [events] that escape its conceptualizing, then it automatically becomes more incidental music such as that with which the SS had tried to drown out the screams of its victims.[26]

It would be wrong to perceive Adorno exclusively as a commentator on Jewish suffering, whose radical criticism of traditional thinking might have been justified in regard to Nazism but which has only limited meaning for the present. The basic elements of our society, the failure of the principles of culture (which became apparent at Auschwitz), have not changed. The menace of collective death is still a possibility in our historical present.

"The secret of his philosophy is the unbelievable dimension of despair,"[27] Adorno writes about Kant's philosophy. This definition could simultaneously be regarded as an accurate description of his own philosophy. Death as the unbearable aspect of life encouraged Kant to posit the metaphysical idea of immortality-as-hope in contradiction to theoretical reasoning; in this "desire to save" he drew conclusions from human suffering which form the condition for Adorno to create a philosophy that is not satisfied with a [simple] affirmative reconstruction of the existing order. Under the existing directives of a goods producing society humans suppress the thought of death so they do not become aware of how far their lives—that have exhausted themselves in the production and consumption of goods—have already come to a standstill. The longing for true resurrection, the most elementary metaphysical interest, is therefore of great importance for nega-

tive dialectics since it points out the significant ideological pretensions of the existing order and since it transcends the close de-
pendency of thought centered on self-preservation by abolishing
the principle of denial.

It [materialism] agrees most with theology where it is most materialistic. Its longing would be the resurrection of the flesh; theology remains alien to idealism, the domain of the absolute Mind.
The escape point of historical materialism would be its own suspension; the liberation of the mind from the priority of material
needs by satisfying the needs. The mind would be reconciled after these needs are satisfied and it would remain so only as long
as it refuses the [continued] satisfaction of material needs as a victim of the materialistic conditions.[28]

The idea of objective truth, which negative dialectics attempts
to determine, lies beyond the need for the identity that the logic
of absolutized self-preservation has put on subjects (as well as
objects).

Dialectics is the self-consciousness of an objectively distorted context, from which it has not yet escaped... However, the absolute,
as metaphysics tries to imply, would be the "non-identical" that
would only reveal itself after the need for identity had
vanished...It is the determination of negative dialectics that it
is not satisfied by and of itself as if it were absolute; that is its form
and expression of hope.[29]

7

ADORNO'S *AESTHETIC THEORY*

by Hans-Martin Lohmann

Those of Adorno's writings that deal extensively with aesthetic subjects and configurations (namely his music and literary theories and his musical and literary sociology) take an important place in his total work, not only regarding their quantity but also their quality. It is quite obvious that Adorno's aesthetic reflections do not belong to a different category of theorizing apart from his philosophy and social science. One can, with good reason, believe that his probing of aesthetic problems—which is particularly developed in his *Aesthetic Theory* (appearing posthumously in fragments in 1970)—forms the theoretical synthesis of all his work. It is to this work that I shall primarily refer in the following.

Adorno's *Aesthetic Theory* is, beside *Negative Dialectics*, his "actual philosophical legacy,"[1] something "that I can throw onto the scales."[2] This, however, requires a clarification of why somebody who saw himself as a Marxist—although a critical one—would retreat to a philosophical field that Marxists generally view as the "side-show" of class conflict. Why would he get involved with "art" when the laws of capitalist production and exchange values form the actual nexus of social intercourse and thus the *nervus rerum* for a critical theory of society?

Adorno, like almost all representatives of Critical Theory (especially Horkheimer, Marcuse, Löwenthal, Benjamin, von Borkenau and Wittfogel), had increasing doubt that the proletariat, the designated subject of historical progress, could any longer be the addressee of the theory of emancipation. This perspective established itself at the end of the 1930's and was constituted by two fundamental experiences: the terroristic establishment of fascism, which maintained the capitalistic production system in Western Europe and the development of Stalinistic terror in the Soviet Union. In 1942 Adorno writes:

> The total organization of society through big business and its omnipresent technology has penetrated the world and the imagination so completely that to think of a different world has become an almost hopeless effort. The devilish picture of harmony, the invisibility of the classes petrified in their circumstances, will gain real control over our consciousness because the idea that the oppressed, the proletarians of all countries, might unify as one class, seems to be hopeless."[3] Due to the "levelling of mass society"[4] that did not weaken social control but rather cemented it to unrecognizability, even the mere mentioning of proletariat, solidarity and class war has become a lie for Critical Theory.[5]

The proletariat is more and more replaced by a small group of intellectuals or even by the "solitary"[6] intellectual who doesn't see himself as subject to progress but rather as a critical institution of remembrance and reflection which recognizes and digests the conditions of defeat and ruin of the former revolutionary class. The intellectuals are the "last enemies of the citizens and, at the same time, the last citizens"; they are privileged to think and to recognize that which releases them from "the naked reproduction of existence" yet, this also indicates "the paltriness of their privilege."[7]

Fascism and Stalinism have proven that "the proletariat" is a fiction in the revolutionary sense of Marx's theory because all attempts at revolutionary liberation—like those in Russia in 1917 and in Germany in 1918-19—were "suspended" through state bureaucracy or counter-revolutions. Thus, Adorno concludes that it is only the solitary theoretician (or the artist) who will withstand the "pressure of conformity."[8] Critical Theory must dissociate itself from the proletariat and from the classic revolutionary concepts of Marx. In the same way Critical Theory must dissociate itself from the belief in the West (and the East) that science and technology provide humanizing results. Since the 1940's, Marxist positions and theorems are, therefore, only casually mentioned in Adorno's and Horkheimer's version of the Critical Theory. The center of its efforts is now the "criticism of instrumental reason" related to the true epochal interrelations of control; criticism has nothing else to do but to catch up with the failed course of evolution.[9]

To reorientate or reformulate critical social theory, which must now see its essential work in tracking the "pathogenesis of occidental rationality,"[10] implicates the transformation of the revolutionary theory into a negative historical philosophy. It is negative in a way that the socio-economic conditions defined by Marx as positive prerequisites to erase the bourgeois class system have indeed not disappeared but have become theoretically unimportant in view of the "spell" of instrumental reason that has become an indifferent, non-transparent system of control; giving the existence of a subject that has control over itself the appearance of a chimera.

This diagnosis, of course, is only possible after experiencing the failing of revolutionary liberation attempts: it converges with historically earlier experiences which needed the "aesthetic" expression, as in the case of Adorno. That social theory becomes aesthetic, that camouflaged politics appear in the robe of beauty is the essential story of modern history; the aesthetic opposition believing against the bourgeois—then later Marxist—idea of progress is a central theme since the French revolution. We find this theme, in its early and radical stages, in early romanticism with Novalis and F. Schlegel who found themselves confronting a historical constellation at the turn of the 18th century that was analogous to the situation, in some points, of the Critical Theory at the end of the 1930's. The affinity of Adorno's theory to texts of the early romantics—an affinity that Adorno acknowledges in the "virtuously displayed gesture of esoteric insinuation"[11]—is by no means accidental:

> The history of Critical Theory and also of neo-Marxism in general, is the renaissance of Marxists adopting early-romantic insights. Early-romantic and also neo-Marxist aestheticism react seismographically to the experience of failing revolutions. Early-romantic and also neo-Marxist criticism of the critical theory of subjectivity understand themselves as sorrowful memories of the fact that the right times had been missed in 1789 and 1917/1918."[12]

The early-romantic retreat to an "aesthetic subject," to an "aesthetic absolutism"[13]—poetry as an incantation to a "negative place of salvation"[14]—gains substance predominantly from the understanding that modern-rational programs of enlightenment and revolution will fail or turn false because they hypostatize a subjectivity which is said to control itself. Yet, this "is" a hypostasis if one can show that the terminological use of "reason," as established by idealistic philosophy, derives from a fundamental misappropriation: the resulting synthesis of the subject of reason is, in fact, a synthesis accomplished by the universal exchange of merchandise and the universality of money;[15] this understanding can be found with Novalis, and also, 40 years later, with Marx:

> Money is the general, self-constituted value of all things. It has, therefore, deprived the whole world, the human world and also nature, of its properties. Money, the essence of his work and his being, is alien to man, and this alien creature controls him and he worships it.[16]

The claim to autonomy and general recognition postulated by the subject of reason of modern history proves to be the "cover up"[17] of the fact that money and valid rules derive from one social logic—the transsubjective logic of the exchange of equivalents. In this respect, modern revolutions are only an expression of a superindividual social reasoning that forcibly identifies everything else to its own interpretation and forces it under its control.

Both the early romantics and Adorno react to this experience. The program of rational criticism cannot, however, develop in a social vacuum; it indeed needs a medium that does not simply dispose of existing reason; with the help of its aesthetic subversion it should rather call attention to its deficient mode and thus finally bring it to its actual existence. This medium constitutes art (both for the early romantics and for Adorno) and the central concept that could undermine reason—already limited by rationality—is Schelling's "intellectual view."[18] With the help of this concept which was also used by Schlegel ("the intellectual view is the Categorical Imperative of Theory")[19] it is perhaps possible to work out an important aspect of Adorno's Aesthetic Theory.

The term "Aesthetic Theory" is as ambiguous as the term "intellectual view." The term "theory" implies that the subjects dealt with are determined by reason; on the other hand, aesthetics themselves cannot be determined by reason: "Fortunately, works of art need not endure. . . ."[20] their immanent telos, according to Adorno, is to withstand the pressure of the categorical purposes of reason. If *Aesthetic Theory* and its subject—art—are, on the one hand, intellectual and provided that they don't simply deny reason but rather absorb it in its substance (in numerous places Adorno speaks of the "spirit of the works of art"[21]. .) they still point beyond subjects that are purely determined by reason in the way that they concentrate on the clear, concrete and predetermined. Between spontaneous immediateness and the highest intellectuality works of art have found their place.

Yet, one still encounters another difficulty when focusing on the title of Adorno's main work. One must ask: Does *Aesthet ic Theory* talk about the "theory of the aesthetic" (*genetivus ob-*

jectivus) or is *Aesthetic Theory* a "theory that is aesthetic" (*genetivus subjectivus*)? The one remains as unclear as the other and we probably have to resign ourselves to the thought that *Aesthetic Theory* in its entirety has something of a rebus riddle about it that nobody has yet been able to decipher. When reading through this very contradictory work[22] one must necessarily settle with picking out a particular, subjective aspect without guarantee that this is the main topic—if one indeed follows Adorno's dictum about art towards his own work: that everything is "equally close to the center"[23] or everything is equally far away.

Adorno proceeds from the quite romantic idea that works of art are the only, and so to speak, last refuge of a subversive uncompromised subject. Therefore, he defends art quite stubbornly against those from the left who despise art[24]; yet, meanwhile, even they have realized that an end of bourgeois art has been predicted too hastily. Art is the place for Adorno at which the "separation of sensuality and understanding"[25] is suspended through the fact that "spiritualization and obsession" are combined through "what is farthest from intellectuality"[26] and supposedly nowhere else realizable. Yet, it is that "distance from intellectuality" that seems to fascinate Adorno more than the domestication and civilization of the chaos in art, caused by the "mind." One can read *Aesthetic Theory* psychoanalytically as a coded theory of desire that speaks out on what has been discarded by individuals on their evolutionary path to civilization. Adorno does indeed speak of the necessary "progressive intellectualization" of works of art[27] which would then become the index of their modernity; he is also aware of the connection between criticism of culture and barbarity [28] but those insights are always attacked by those who see the mind as simply heteronomous, while the occidental need for thought and abstraction is a treason on "the untamed pre-egotistical impulse."[29] The conditions of freedom which Adorno focuses on and which he sees in reality in successful works of art allow movements in the subject which destroy and diffuse identity. Affinity to what lies remote from intellectuality, as it is expressed in *Negative Dialectics*, "is the apex of enlightened dialectics"[30] and, if the work of art realizes such affinity in itself, namely "to annihilate the spell of being dispersed by the subject,"[31] then it is the carrier of a desire which individuals in ecstasy about their pretended autonomy and self-certainty have denied themselves.

With good reason one can observe[32] that the late version of Critical Theory—its beginning announced by the *Dialectics of Enlightenment*, while its most mature and darkest product is the *Aesthetic Theory*—agrees in many aspects with the expression of French structuralism's criticism of reason and the subject. In fact, enough proof can be found in Aesthetic Theory that Adorno took very seriously the idea that the transcendental-philosophical subject can find its realization in a bold move against its nature. This constitutes the hedonic and pleasure-emphasizing character of this work: the destruction of the subject and its "meaning" is done in the name of an artistic subjectivity that reveals its different character unceremoniously without falling for it blindly. "Art is not nature but it wants to redeem what nature promises."[33] Structuralism, as in the version by Foucault[34], has revealed that a subject's focus on reason is a self-deception and the result of extremes; likewise Adorno deciphers the decentrism of any meaning in the advanced productions of modern art: "The more radical works of art draw their conclusions from the state of consciousness the closer they get to absurdity."[35] In such wording we find not only a perception but also a desire: the desire to take back the rational single-meaningness of instrumental reason which will truly mean the destruction of reason, as Adorno keeps reminding us. "Because identity will not be the last word of reason,"[36] because anti-social[37] manifestations of art carry along in their manifold meanings the "mortgage of what was left behind, of the regressive"[38] as a promise, therefore art fights against the need of reason for control to keep the repressed desire, after a "suspension of the *Ich*,"[39] in its threatening state of separation.

When *Aesthetic Theory* emphasizes art's "language remote

of meaning" and, with that, its aspects which diffuse and destroy meaning then it probably corresponds with the objective social circumstances more than all [other] statements which grant art a somewhat positive "function" and thus form hopes and expectations which Adorno denies rigorously any right for existence: "For the sake of reconciliation the authentic works must destroy any reminders of reconciliation."[40] As "summary of truth,"[41] not as "the" truth or any approximation of it, art provides a truth of higher order—as "secular governor of the old religion"[42]—which systematically disregards the "rules of a 'police' that watches every term used."[43]

It is true that *Aesthetic Theory* is, so to speak, an "episodic absence in the rational progress of the Modern" which, as H. Timm stated regarding the early-romantics,[44] "says the truth in the world of turmoil"[45]; however, at the same time one must emphasize that Adorno puts a tight terminological rein on his desire theory: he tames it, so to speak. The French desire theoreticians (headed by Foucault and Deleuze/Guattari) who see their work in deconstruction as an intention to give the falling subject of meaning, "the master of speech," a final malicious push, do not have a reliable ally in Adorno. "Blindness against right reason," as he writes in *Nervenpunkte der neuen Musik*, "or the sacrifice of meaning in favor of action has become so popular that one is suspected of romantic backwardness when one actually reflects on the reason in art."[46] Adorno will not allow, by any means, the structuralist notion that the autonomous subject is simply a grandiose self-deception. M. Frank has justly pointed out that there is indeed a similarity between the conversion of desperation into cheerfulness and the neurotic "conversion to optimism" which Sartre had analyzed in Flaubert.[47] Adorno's *Aesthetic Theory* has no room for optimism and Balzac's formula remains valid for him: "Whoever says poetry means sorrow."

The difference between Adorno and the cheery positivism of the structuralists lies in Adorno's term "second reflection"[49] which does not necessarily want to get rid of reason but rather

intends to gain more freedom for the object in the name of its
own potential. Therefore, Adorno criticizes those ideas which attempt salvation in pure immediacy and clarity.

> The anamnesis of freedom in natural beauty misleads because it
> hopes to find freedom in the unfree. The naturally beautiful is the
> myth that was transposed into the imagination and through that
> satisfies. Everyone considers the singing of birds to be beautiful;
> there is no one with European roots who wouldn't be touched
> by the sound of a blackbird after a rain. Yet, in the singing of the
> birds lurks the horrible because the singing is not singing but rather
> the birds obey the spell that was cast on them... only what would
> have escaped from nature as fate would help nature restore itself.[49]

One can compare Adorno's asceticism against the unchecked
principle of pleasure which is propagated by some of the recent
French Philosophers, along with Freud's position. Freud was a
frontrunner, like no one else before or after, for the liberation
of lust, sexuality and sensuality. But his program stood its ground
that "It" should become "I." Adorno's *Aesthetic Theory* partici-
pates in this understanding of reason that has seen through its
own limitations and its conditioning by society. *Aesthetic Theory*
does not give a free ticket to those apostles of sensuality who
mistake secondary nature for the first; nor does it lend any proof
to the champions of the existing reason. *Aesthetic Theory* is dark
because it denies any claim to truthkeeping:"art's claim to truth
and its affinity to the untrue are one."[50] This is also valid for the
Aesthetic Theory. This is exactly what causes the problem. It is
recommended to the reader who dares to get into this most
difficult and most contradictory of all of Adorno's texts, to use
it as an introduction and to follow as a pattern what Adorno had
seen united in aesthetic behavior: Eros and Cognition.[51]

NOTES

CW - Refers to the Collected Works of T. Adorno published in German by Suhrkamp Verlag, Frankfurt 1970

1. For an account of the early history of the Frankfurt School see: Buck-Morris, *The Origin Of Negative Dialectics*, New York, 1977
2. CW - Vol.1, p.334
3. Ibid, p.340
4. Ibid, p.335
5. Ibid, p.336
6. Ibid
7. CW - Vol.5, p.141
8. CW - Vol.1, p.345
9. Ibid, p.362 (see also p. 354)
10. Ibid, p.360
11. Ibid, p. 358
12. Ibid, p.354
13. Ibid
14. CW - Vol.6, p.352
15. CW - Vol.1, p.339
16. Ibid, p.365
17. "Reflections On the Class Theory" in CW, Vol.8
18. Found in CW, Vol.11
19. CW - Vol.5
20. Ibid, p.20
21. Ibid, p.32
22. Horkheimer/Adorno *Dialektik der Aufklärung*, Amsterdam, 1947 p.5
23. CW - Vol.5, p.32
24. Ibid, p.33

25. Ibid, p.34
26. Ibid, p.37
27. See H. Ebeling, *Subjektivität und Selbsterhaltung*, Frankfurt,1976
28. A. Kojéve, *Hegel*, Frankfurt, 1975,p.58
29. See also E.Cassirer, *Die Philosophie der Aufklärung*, Tubingen,1932; P. Gay, *The Enlightenment*, London, 1968
30. Horkheimer/Adorno, *Dialektik der Aufklärung*, p.19
31. See Adorno, et.al. *Die Positivismusstreit in der deutsschen Soziologie*, Neuwied/Berlin 1969; also U. Baeck, *Objektivität und Normativität*, Reinbeck 1974
32. T. Parsons, *The Social System*, p.101
33. Adorno, *Der Positivismusstreit*, p.21
34. Ibid
35. See G. Skirbek, *Wahreitstheorien*, Frankfurt, 1977
36. Adorno, *Der Positivismusstrteit*, p. 36

Negative Dialectics
by P. Schiefelbein

1. CW - Vol.6, p.10
2. Ibid, p.43
3. Ibid, p.9
4. Ibid, p.10
5. Ibid, p.21
6. Ibid, p.148
7. Ibid, p.66
8. Ibid, p.165
9. CW - Vol.1 p.366-371
10. Ibid, p.369
11. CW - 6, p.19
12. Ibid, p.55
13. Ibid, p.29
14. Ibid, p.164
15. Ibid, p.50
16. Ibid, p.21
17. Ibid, p.61
18. CW - Vol.6, p.166
19. Ibid, p.39
20. Ibid, p.347
21. Ibid, p.96
22. Ibid, p.390
23. Ibid, p.391
24. Ibid, p.358
25. Ibid, p.355
26. Ibid, p.358
27. Ibid, p.378
28. Ibid, p.207
29. Ibid, p.398

Adorno's Aesthetics
by H-M Lohmann

1. R. Bubner "Kann Theorie ästhetisch werden? Zum Haupt- motiv der Philosophie Adornos", in B. Lindner/W.M. Lüdke (eds.) *Materialien zur ästhetischen Theorie. Theodor W. Adornos Konstruktion der Moderne*, Frankfurt,1980 p.109
2. CW - Vol.7, p.537
3. CW - Vol.8, p.376
4. Ibid
5. T. Adorno, *Minima Moralia*, Frankfurt, 1969 p.146
6. Ibid, p.22; see also H. Dubiel, *Wissenschaftsorganisation und politische Erfahrung. Studien zur frühen Kritischen Theorie*, Frankfurt, 1978, p.100
7. Adorno, *Minima Moralia*, p.24
8. Ibid, p.26
9. See the discussion on Odysseus in Horkheimer/Adorno *Dialektik der Aufklärung*
10. J.Hörisch, "Herrschewort, Geld und geltende Sätze. Adornos Aktualisierung der Frühromantik und ihre Affinität zur poststrukturalistischen Kritik des Subjekts", In Lindner/Ludke (eds.) p. 339
11. Ibid, p.400
12. Ibid
13. See B. Lypp *Ästhetischer Absolutismus un politische Vernunft. Zum Widerstreit von Reflexionen und Sittlichkeit im deutschen Idealismus*, Frankfurt, 1972
14. M. Frank, *Die undendliche Fahrt.Ein Motiv und sein Text*, Frankfurt, 1979. p.14
15. See the works of A. Sohn-Rethel, particularly *Geistige und körperliche Arbeit. Zur Theorie der gesellschaftlichen Synthesis*, Frankfurt, 1970
16. K. Marx, "Zur Judenfrage" in Marx/Engels, Collected Works, Berlin, 1957 Vol.1,p.375
17. Hörisch, p.404
18. F.W.J. Schelling, *System des transzendentalen Idealismus*, Hamburg, 1958, p.37
19. F. Schlegel *Schriften zur Literatur*, München 1972, p.32
20. CW - Vol.7, p.30
21. Ibid, p.228
22. See K.M. Michel "Versuch die 'Ästhetische Theorie' zu vertehen" In Lindner/Lüdke (eds.),p.41

23. CW - Vol.7 p.228; see also p.156
24. Ibid, p.372
25. Ibid, p.260
26. Ibid, p.144
27. Ibid, p.141
28. See Adorno *Negative Dialektik*, Frankfurt, 1966 p.359
29. Ibid, p.219
30. Ibid, 264
31. CW - Vol.7, p.203
32. See Hörisch, p.408
33. CW - Vol.7, p.103
34. See M. Foucault Die Ordnung des Diskurses, München, 1974
35. CW - Vol.7, p.506
36. Ibid, p.100
37. See Ibid, p.335, 348
38. Ibid, p.487
39. CW - Vol.11, p.79
40. CW - Vol.7, p.348
41. Ibid, p.391
42. Frank, p.14
43. Foucault, p.25
44. H. Timm, *Die heilige Revolution, Das religiöse Totalitätskonzept der Frühromantik*, Frankfurt, 1978 p.14
45. Foucault, p.14
46. Adorno, *Nervenpunkte der neuen Musik*, Reinbeck, 1969, p.96
47. M. Frank, *Das Sagbare und das Unsagbare. Studien zur neuesten französischen Hermeneutik und Texttheorie*, Frankfurt, 1980 p.37,108
48. CW - Vol.7, p.105
49. Ibid, p.104
50. Ibid, p.403
51. Ibid, p.490

SELECTED BIBLIOGRAPHY

Major Works by Adorno in English

Aesthetic Theory, trans. C. Lenhardt (London and New York, 1984)
Against Epistemology: A Metacritique, trans. W. Domingo, (Cambridge, 1984)
Dialectic of Enlightenment with M. Horkheimer, trans. J Cumming, (New York, 1972)
In Search of Wagner, trans. R. Livingstone (London, 1981)
Introduction to the Sociology of Music, trans. E.B. Ashton (New York, 1976)
The Jargon of Authenticity, trans. K. Tarnowski and F. Will (London, 1973)
Minima Moralia, trans. E.F.N. Jephcott, (London, 1974)
Negative Dialectics, trans. E.B. Ashton, (New York, 1973)
Prisms, trans. Samuel and Shierry Weber, (Cambridge, 1981)

Several Works About Adorno in English

Buck-Morss, S. *The Origin of Negative Dialectics: Theodor W. Adorno, Walter Benjamin and the Frankfurt Institite* (New York, 1977)
Jameson, F. *Late Marxism: Adorno, Or, The Persistence of the Dialectic* (London-New York, 1990)
Jay, Martin *Adorno* (Cambridge, 1984)
Rose, Gillian *The Melancholy Science: an Introduction to the Thought of Theodor W. Adorno* (New York, 1978)

See Also

Arato, A. and Gebhardt.E. (eds.) *Essential Frankfurt School Reader* (New York and Oxford, 1978)
Jay, Martin *The Dialectical Imagination: A History of the Frankfurt School and the Institute of Social Research 1923-1950* (Boston, 1973)

Lunn, Eugene *Marxism and Modernism: An Historical Study of Lukàcs, Brecht, Benjamin and Adorno* (Berkeley, 1982)
O' Neill, J. (ed.) *On Critical Theory* (New York, 1976)
Tar, Zoltan *The Frankfurt School: The Critical Theories of Max Horkhaimer and Theodor W. Adorno* (New York, 1977)
Taylor, R. (Ed. and trans.) *Aesthetics and Politics* (London, 1977)

Several journals also have significant numbers of articles devoted to Adorno and the Frankfurt School:

Telos
New German Critique
New Left Review

CHRONOLOGY TABLE

1903	Adorno is born in Frankfurt on Sept. 11 to a prosperous wine merchant named Oskar Wiesengrund and his wife of Corsican ancestry whose maiden name was Adorno. Adorno's mother had been an accomplished concert singer and undoubtedly had an influence on his lifelong musical interests and development.
	During his school years at the Frankfurt Gymnasium Adorno befriends the essayist and film theorist Siegfried Kracauer. Together they read Kant's *Critique of Pure Reason*.
1921	Passes *abitur*. Reads Bloch's *Spirit of Utopia* and Lukács *Theory of the Novel*.
1922	Adorno begins his University studies and works in the areas of musical theory and music criticism. In a seminar on Husserl, Adorno befriends Max Horkheimer and shortly thereafter, Walter Benjamin.
1924	Adorno writes a doctoral thesis on Husserl for his teacher Cornelius.
1925/28	Adorno travels to Vienna to study with the composer Alban Berg. While in Vienna he frequently attends the lectures of Karl Kraus and falls under the spell of Vienna's musical avant-garde that was most explicitly defined by Schönberg's experiments in atonality.
1929/30	Assumes editorship of the journal *Anbrach*.
1931	Adorno is back in Germany and begins his post-doctoral thesis under the supervision of Paul Tillich. His inaugural lecture as a professor, "The Actuality of Philosophy," shows the definite influence of Benjamin.

1933	Adorno's post-doctoral study on Kierkegaard appears on January 30, the day Hitler siezed power.
1934	Adorno emigrates to England and begins his tenure at Merton College, Oxford. Here he returns to his studies of Husserl and writes the first draft of a work that will later appear as *Against Epistemology*.
1937	Marries Gretel Karplus.
1938	Emigrates to the United States, changes his name officially from Wiesengrund to Adorno, and assumes an assistant directorship with the Princeton University Radio Research project.
1940	Walter Benjamin commits suicide on the French-Spanish border while trying to leave France.
1941	Adorno moves to California along with Max Horkheimer.
1944	Adorno participates in a large scale research project on the origins of fascism that is co-sponsored by the American Jewish Committee and the Berkeley Public Opinion Study Group.
1949	Adorno returns to Germany with Horkheimer.
1951	Institute for Social Research reopens in Frankfurt.
1952	Adorno returns briefly to the United States to conduct research on popular culture for the Hacker Foundation.
1958	Assumes the directorship of the Institute for Social Research.
1969	Adorno dies on Aug. 6 in Switzerland.

Willem van Reijen is Professor of Philosophy at the University of Utrecht (Netherlands). He has published widely on the subject of Critical Theory.